REFLECTIONS
ON
ISLAM

REFLECTIONS
ON
ISLAM

IDEAS, OPINIONS, ARGUMENTS

GEORGE JONAS

KEY PORTER BOOKS

Library and Archives Canada Cataloguing in Publication

Jonas, George, 1935–

   Reflections on Islam : ideas, opinions, arguments / George Jonas.

ISBN 978-1-55263-886-6

   1. Islam—21st century.   2. Islam and world politics.   3. Civilization, Islamic—21st century. 4. Civilization, Western—21st century.   I. Title.

BP161.3.J65 2007   297.09'051   C2006-906414-8

The publisher gratefully acknowledges the support of the Canada Council for the Arts and the Ontario Arts Council for its publishing program. We acknowledge the support of the Government of Ontario through the Ontario Media Development Corporation's Ontario Book Initiative.

We acknowledge the financial support of the Government of Canada through the Book Publishing Industry Development Program (BPIDP) for our publishing activities.

Key Porter Books Limited
Six Adelaide Street East, Tenth Floor
Toronto, Ontario
Canada M5C 1H6

www.keyporter.com

Text design: Martin Gould
Electronic formatting: Jean Lightfoot Peters

Printed and bound in Canada

07 08 09 10 11 5 4 3 2 1

CONTENTS

2004

2005

2006

ACKNOWLEDGEMENTS

Except for "The Wounded Stork" and "Letter to a Liberal Friend," both of which appear in their present form here for the first time, these reflections on Islam were originally published between 2001 and 2006 in the *National Post*, in syndication for Southam (later CanWest) News Service, and United Press International. I wish to thank editors Natasha Hassan, Jonathan Kay, Douglas Kelly, John O'Sullivan, and Kenneth Whyte for inviting me to write them.

I am indebted to Barbara Amiel for having cast an editorial eye on these pieces as they were being written (as she did on most of my work over the years). I should also note that these essays would not have appeared as newspaper columns without a venue being provided for them, first by Conrad Black, and then by the late Israel Asper and his sons, Leonard and David. I am grateful to them all.

All pieces appear here as originally written. I have changed nothing and added only the titles (the original columns were headlined and edited by the various newspapers in which they appeared). This was not only to preserve the journalistic record, but because it seemed unnecessary to update them. The more things changed in the world since I wrote these pieces, the more they remained the same.

—GJ, Toronto, 2006

REFLECTIONS
ON
ISLAM

LETTER TO A LIBERAL FRIEND

Dear Heather,

Thanks for an enjoyable lunch; thanks for asking me about a liberal response to militant Islam; and thanks for letting me use my reply as a foreword to this collection.

For liberals, it goes against the grain to think in terms of groups rather than individuals. It goes against the grain even more to consider entire ethnic, racial, or religious groups as hostile. It especially goes against the grain to think of other groups as morally or intellectually flawed.

This is a good thing.

The bad thing is that this reluctance sometimes stands in the way of a sober and factual analysis. In recent years it has prevented many liberals from facing certain facts about Islamism and Islam, including the relationship between the two.

Islam is one of the world's great religions. Islamism is a radical movement of intolerance, coercion, and terror. The followers of Islam are a billion faithful Muslims around the world. The followers of Islamism include Osama bin Laden and his al Qaeda, Sheik Omar and his Taliban, the nuclear ayatollahs of theocratic Iran, the militants of Hezbollah, the Armed Islamic Group of Algeria, the late Shamil Basayev's human bombs from Chechnya, and a string of other terrorists in far-flung parts of the globe.

Unfortunately, they also include some of our neighbours down the block or around the corner.

Is there a connection between Islamism and Islam? Liberals wince when someone poses this question.

Whatever the answer, the question is legitimate and liberal-minded people should not have to wince when they hear it. It should not be a taboo for liberals to examine the ideas that fuel some ethnic or religious groups from time to time. It should not be a taboo to examine them honestly and rigorously. It can be a matter of survival to accurately assess historical trends, even when they are associated with ethnic or religious groups. In this, as in most other matters, it is possible to retain liberal principles without losing one's judgment and common sense.

It is a good thing to make sure that we do no injustice to any individual, no matter what group he or she belongs to. It is a good thing to safeguard liberal values. It is a good thing to keep searching our souls.

It is a bad thing to abdicate to evil.

There is no dispute about Islam being one of the world's great religions, a faith that, in the words of the Princeton scholar Bernard Lewis, "has brought comfort and peace of mind to countless millions of men and women." There is equally little doubt, however, about the existence of a less benevolent strain in Islam, which periodically comes to the fore. To quote Professor Lewis again, "Islam, like other religions, has also known periods when it inspired in some of its followers a mood of hatred and violence."

Until the first attack against the World Trade Center in New York in 1993, this hatred was noted in our part of the world mainly by some scholars, some diplomats, a few journalists, and perhaps a handful of intelligence officers. It may have also been noted by the relatives and friends of 241 U.S. Marines killed outside Beirut, Lebanon, when their barracks were blown up in 1983, or by the American hostages in Iran. Dubbed "Muslim rage," at first glance it seemed to be directed primarily against "the great Satan" America and "the little Satan" Israel.

But anti-Americanism and anti-Zionism turned out to be only the tip of the iceberg. The baffling Islamist rage targeted modernity itself, the entire set of ideals and accomplishments of Western civilization and liberal democracy. It was a backlash against the secular values of the contemporary world—a backlash against what Islamists considered the evils of a godless society, with all its licentious customs and indulgences, as viewed from the perspective of the medieval mind.

In the spring of 2001, radical Islamists blew up two gigantic Buddha statutes in the Hindu Kush. Their action made no sense in the twenty-first century but in the eleventh it would have. The Taliban's vandalism was a postcard from the Middle Ages: "Hi, wish you were here!" Crusaders might well have done something similar in their days, except Christendom has come a fair distance since the Crusades. Fundamentalist Islam has not. By the definition of the Dark Ages, those who are not of our faith are infidels, and infidels are the enemies of God. In this view, non-Muslims are infidels. Granted this premise, anything goes. No wonder the militants of radical Islam find it permissible blow up cultural artifacts as they have done in Afghanistan, or commuter trains, as they have done in Madrid. Or to lob mortar shells into kindergartens, as they have done in Israel, or fly hijacked airliners into office buildings, as they have done in New York. One does not show mercy to the enemies of God.

Islamism is not Islam. The two are not to be equated. But is there something about Islam that is conducive to the formation of extremist sects and radical movements? Is Islam a petri dish in which a culture of fundamentalism thrives?

Arguably, yes. Some creeds are friendlier to the separation between a social and a spiritual realm than others. The notion of separating Church and State is rooted in Christianity, where it is expressed as rendering unto Caesar the things that are Caesar's and unto God the things that are God's. This notion is absent in Islam. For Muslims, all things belong to God, including the State. Separation amounts to sacrilege. Such a civilization may discern any manifestation of modernity an assault on its beliefs. If certain secular values—say, equality for women—contradict some tenets of the faith, not being able to separate the things that are Caesar's (or civil society's) from the things that are God's, is more likely to invite a radical response.

All religions have, or have had, radical phases. All religions contain passages of darkness and light in their holy books. It is revealing, though, that after the collapse of the Ottoman Empire the young Turks of Mustafa Kemal Atatürk considered it necessary to suppress Islam in order to modernize Turkey. Kemal has been quoted as describing Islam a "theology of an immoral Arab" and "a dead thing," which "might have suited tribes in the desert," but was "no good for a modern, progressive state." The founder of present-day Turkey even prohibited some items of traditional clothing, such as the fez. The point is not that the young Turks were necessarily right; the point is only that they were Muslims—Muslims who wanted Turkey to progress, and who felt, rightly or wrongly, that Islam was incompatible with modernity.

Islam was more than a religion from the beginning; it was also a political faction and a force. As such, it has been struggling with the non-Islamic world for supremacy for the last 1,400 years. It is important to note that for the first thousand years of this struggle Islam had been triumphant. The crescent moon has been waning only during the last three or four centuries. The gradual ebbing of the Islamic tide created the illusion that the conflict was coming to an end. Three generations in North America and in Europe, including our parents and our grandparents, experienced the mirage of a lull in the ancient struggle. The calm between the collapse of the Ottoman Empire (1918) and the collapse of the Peacock Throne of Iran (1979) was especially deceptive. When Islam's jihad resumed after the fall of the Persian shah in 1979, it caught many, if not most, Westerners by surprise. This subject will be explored in the pages that follow.

Many people think of the Middle East as the main battleground between militant Islam and the non-Islamic world. There is even a view that the central conflict is between Israel and the Palestinians. If that conflict could be resolved, the problems of radical Islam, terrorism, and so on, would go away or at least be greatly reduced. Nothing could be farther from the truth. "Wherever one looks along the perimeter of Islam, Muslims have problems living peaceably with their neighbours," wrote Harvard professor Samuel Huntington in his much-quoted *The Clash of Civilizations and the Remaking of World Order*. Settling the Israeli-Palestinian conflict would be important and desirable. But it is not the root cause of the clash between the Islamic and non-Islamic world. It is only one conflict among many. Iranian theocracy, Saudi Wahhabism, or Pakistani-Afghan talibanism have nothing to do with the creation of the Jewish state. Such flashpoints as Kashmir, Chechnya, Kosovo, Xinjiang, and North Maluku are very distant from the conflicts of the Middle East. More about that later in this book.

What is the liberal response to Islam's sentimental journey to the Middle Ages?

After Malaysian prime minister Mahathir Mohamad made crudely anti-Semitic remarks at an international conference in 2003, fifty-seven world leaders applauded him. Canada's then prime minister, Jean Chrétien, shook Dr. Mahathir's hand after his speech without a hint of censure. Dr. Mahathir said things for which people in Canada have been prosecuted—and Canada's Liberal prime minister shook hands with him.

At Montreal's Concordia University, administrators were faced with a simple choice: they could support students who wished to exercise their right to freedom of assembly and expression by inviting a former Israeli prime minister to speak, or a pro-Palestinian mob who threatened to curtail this right by violence. University authorities chose to support the bullies, not once but twice. After the first episode, when former Israeli prime minister Benjamin "the

Hawk" Netanyahu was prevented from speaking, there was considerable public outrage. The Manhattan Institute's Abigail Thernstrom called Concordia "an island of repression in a sea of freedom." Two years later, when former Israeli prime minister Ehud "the Dove" Barak was also prevented from speaking, there was mainly silence. Canadians were getting used to repression. The sea of freedom was receding. It seemed no longer navigable.

After Netanyahu was stopped from speaking, the university governors, in a twisted show of "even-handedness," imposed a temporary moratorium on all Middle East debates. I commented in a column: "In a country based on such principles as freedom of inquiry and freedom of association, a university can't do the right thing by silencing both sides in a debate; it can only do the right thing by enabling both sides to speak. Political sympathies for one side or another are neither here nor there. In a liberal democracy, the authorities must support the side that wishes to exercise its fundamental right to speak and assemble against the side that would prevent it by intimidation and force."

Toronto's York University came close to cancelling a speech by the Philadelphia-based scholar, Daniel Pipes. Dr. Pipes is viewed as pro-Israel. Under pressure from pro-Palestinian students and faculty, York's student government withdrew permission for use of the campus pub where Dr. Pipes was scheduled to speak. Canadians who wished to hear the American scholar could do so only in a curtained-off corner of a basketball court and after going through metal detectors. Later Dr. Pipes described the scene in the *National Post*: "Several bodyguards took me through a back entrance to the gym and sequestered me in a holding room until I entered the gym.... But surely the most memorable aspect of this talk was the briefing by James Hogan, a detective in the Hate Crime Unit of the Toronto Police Service, to make sure I was aware that Canada's Criminal Code makes a variety of public statements actionable, including advocating genocide and promoting hatred of a specific group."

My comment was: "The sheer audacity of this takes one's breath away. Cops lecturing a scholar on the law against hate crimes before letting him into an auditorium is like cops lecturing a shopper on the law against shoplifting before letting him into a department store.... By subjecting Dr. Pipes to Detective Hogan's briefing, for no other conceivable reason than that he's a scholar of Jewish background with pro-Israeli views, it was the Toronto Police that came closest to committing a hate crime that day."

Liberal societies have tried to accommodate medieval Islamism. We have encouraged those who do not share our values to use our values against us. Our police are not reading the riot act to people who threaten to violently suppress free speech, but to people who try to peacefully exercise it. Unless we recognize and reverse this trend, far from remaking the Middle East in our image, we will come to resemble the Middle East.

Kindest regards,
George Jonas
Toronto, All Hallow's Day, 2006

2001

THE TALIBAN IS A TIME MACHINE

CanWest News Service, March 21, 2001

It's easy to be revolted by the Taliban's destruction of the great Buddha statues of Afghanistan. It's a revulsion I share. Like most people born in the twentieth century, I consider book burnings or the destruction of cultural artifacts nauseating.

But much as I've mixed feelings about defending vandalism, or even appearing to do so, it's useful to recall that the Taliban hasn't invented the practice of smashing artifacts. Many religions abhor competition: it's in their nature. God is a jealous god, and varieties of iconoclasm or book burnings have been with us for a long time.

The Byzantine Empire succeeded the Roman Empire in the east and adopted Christianity. In 391 AD Alexandria's library, a wonder of the ancient world, was destroyed by fire when the Byzantine emperor Theodosius ordered that all non-Christian works must be eliminated. The library was rebuilt, but in the eighth century the caliph Harûn ar-Rashîd, a lifelong enemy of Byzantium, ordered it to be burned again. Perhaps ar-Rashîd did not want to be outdone by Theodosius. According to legend, he remarked that if the books in the library said the same thing as the Koran, they were superfluous, and if they said something else they needed to be destroyed.

Iconoclasm flourished in eighth- and ninth-century Byzantium, favoured by such orthodox Christian emperors as Leo III, though eventually Pope Gregory II excommunicated him for breaking too many things. But the Western Church also had its limits when it came to cultural expression. In the sixteenth century, Pope Paul III issued his *Index Liborum Prohibitorum*, followed by Pope Paul IV's *Index Auctorum et Liborum*, which in 1543 banned books and authors suspected of heresy throughout Christendom. The Church then maintained its index of forbidden literature for centuries. Books and authors "put on the index" became untouchable for faithful Catholics.

The roots of anti-idolatry go back to the Bible. Exodus 20:4–5 records God's Commandments as "Thou shalt not make unto thee any graven image" and "Thou shalt not bow thyself down to them, nor serve them." The cult of false gods and deification of graven images has been decried by all faiths that regard their own dogmas as writ in stone.

Judaism and Christianity traditionally viewed worship of heathen gods and creation of heathen idols as sinful, and often considered iconoclasm as virtuous. The difference between the Taliban and mainstream Judeo-Christianity is time: about six hundred years or so. In the last few centuries—since the Renaissance, more or less—we have made wide-ranging cultural exceptions to our prohibition of idolatry.

The Taliban take religious prohibitions literally. Many fundamentalists, whether in Islam, Judaism, or Christianity, don't consider the handiwork of men (i.e., culture) more important than the commandments of God as set down in their holy books. After all, the Taliban did nothing that Moses did not do when, upon his return from Mount Sinai, with the stone tablets in his hand, he found his people, led by his own brother Aaron, dancing around the Golden Calf.

According to Exodus 33:20, Moses took the calf and burned it, and ground it into powder, and threw it into the water, "and made the children of Israel drink of it."

Should Moses smash the Golden Calf today, we would no doubt regard it as a barbaric destruction of human heritage. We would protect the Golden Calf against the word of God, as brought down from the mountain, carved in stone, by the prophet. This is the choice modern people would make, myself included—except I know that it's a choice with mixed consequences, like all choices.

Take UNESCO's repeated proposal, for instance, that destruction of cultural property be made a war crime. Attractive as this is to all of us who admire architecture, it would have made Allied leaders war criminals for bombing many sites in Germany during World War II. For others, the esthetics of nature may be paramount: environmental activists might call it a crime against humanity to deface pristine country sides with statues, whether in Afghanistan or Mount Rushmore.

It's a pity about the Buddhas of Afghanistan. Yet if one looks at things another way, the Taliban are doing us a cultural service. They have become our time machine. They teleport us back into history; they hold up a magic mirror in which we can see how we ourselves used to think and act until a scant few centuries ago.

THE ENEMIES OF CIVILIZATION

CanWest News Service, September 19, 2001

Last week the media got into the habit of calling the enemies of civilization "unseen" and "faceless." Unseen? Faceless? Their faces have been on TV. Everybody has seen them.

They came in several varieties. They included street mobs of Palestinians demonstrating their hatred for Israel, and street mobs of Pakistanis demonstrating their support for the Taliban. Both cheered the fiery deaths of office workers and airline passengers in the U.S.

Next came a set of talking heads. They weren't necessarily Arab or Muslim, though they included many. They started out with expressions of obligatory regret over the civilian causalities, but then, almost in the same breath, went on to advocate the terrorists' agenda.

They explained that airliners will continue crashing into America's office buildings until the U.S. tailors its foreign policy to the terrorists' taste, and stops supporting Israel or lifts economic sanctions against Iraq. Or until the West abandons Western values, from secular democracy to individual freedom.

Even NBC TV's news anchor, Tom Brokaw, after talking about the need to resist terrorism, added that we must stop "creating pockets of hate" in the world. But it's a liberal fallacy that we "create" pockets of hate. Pockets of hate are being created by fanatics who exploit the envy and resentment of the ignorant.

In his first speech last Tuesday, President George W. Bush said America will not distinguish between those who commit terrorist acts and those who harbour them. Except, ironically, this includes the U.S. and Canada. Most Western countries have harboured and trained terrorists, however unwittingly.

The moral difference is great between witting and unwitting, or even heedless. The practical difference can be negligble.

We've aided and tutored terrorists through alliances abroad, from the Balkans to Afghanistan, as well as through immigration policies and multicultural ideals at home. A report in the *Los Angeles Times* suggests two hijackers were former Saudi fighter pilots who had studied at the Defence Language Institute at Lackland Air Force Base in Texas, and the Air War College at Maxwell Air Force Base, Alabama.* Robert Fife notes in the *National Post* that "[t]he U.S. Congress and the Canadian Security Intelligence Service have warned that virtually every known terrorist organization in the world is exploiting Canada's ethnic communities, posing a serious security threat."

"The face of terror is not the true faith of Islam," remarked President Bush while visiting a mosque. No doubt. The war with terrorism is in many ways "an inter-Islamic struggle," as Clifford Orwin put it in the *National Post*. Taliban-type fundamentalists are fighting with fellow Muslims who prefer enlightened, tolerant societies. This struggle has been going on since the days of Mustafa Kemal Atatürk, who established the modern Republic of Turkey in 1923.

A great tragedy in this conflict is that most members of the Muslim communities in the West have chosen sides a long time ago: they've chosen democracy. Most people from Middle East countries settled in the West because they've made a choice for freedom versus tyranny, enlightenment versus the Middle Ages.

But there's a split, which terrorists exploit in their home countries as well as in immigrant communities. In the

* This was erroneous.

Ottawa Citizen, David Warren describes Osama bin Laden's message as "the need for war, the final war, between the decadent West, and an aroused Islam with a billion soldiers." All of Islam certainly doesn't agree with bin Laden; probably most of Islam doesn't. But some of it does, and more will as the war continues.

Unhappily, this scenario is predictable. Some Muslims will be tempted to jump on the seemingly successful bandwagon of the terrorists. A few will come to believe that the reaction and defensive measures of Western democracies give them no choice.

Places like Pakistan—and to some extent Saudi Arabia or Jordan—have a peculiar problem. The governments in these countries support the West, but many people don't support the governments—at least, not reliably.

Many commentators warn that the war against terrorism shouldn't be perceived as being between the East and the West, or between Islamic and non-Islamic cultures. True enough—but that's how the war is perceived by many on both sides.

Listing these difficulties means only that we'll have to face them, not that we should give in to them. Western-style democracies must stay the course. We shouldn't abandon allies abroad, or civil liberties at home. We shouldn't mistreat fellow citizens of any ethnicity or religion. We should never surrender to the worst impulses of either our enemies or our own.

CLASH OF CIVILIZATIONS?

National Post, October 14, 2001

From news anchors to King Abdullah of Jordan, the mantra is being repeated. This is a war against terrorism, not a war between East and West. It isn't a clash of civilizations. It's not a struggle between the Islamic and non-Islamic world.

Terrorists are eager to present the conflict in a different light. "Wherever there are Americans and Jews, they will be targeted," said a statement issued by Osama bin Laden's al Qaeda organization on Tuesday. "Wherever there are Muslims, they should prepare for jihad, and by the grace of God, the victory will be Islam's."

Pro-Western Islamic states, and even anti-Western ones, carefully distance themselves from such views. Ever since U.S. president George W. Bush declared that America will not distinguish between terrorists and those who harbour them, governments that supported terrorists for decades suddenly discovered that the safest place for them is within the U.S.-led anti-terrorist coalition. From Pakistan—a country that helped create the Taliban and impose it on Afghanistan in the first place—to such rogue states as Syria and Iran, almost every Mideast country is declaring itself against terrorism. Yasser Arafat gave blood on TV, leaving Molière's classic hypocrite, Tartuffe, in the dust. There are no terrorist states outside the coalition by now, except Iraq, Libya, and the Taliban-ruled part of Afghanistan.

Had newcomers to anti-terrorism undergone a genuine change of heart and policy, it would be one thing. In fact, most have only joined for cover, coupled with a hope of trying to sabotage the coalition. As the U.S. administration involves itself with the delicate task of coalition building, it needs to keep in mind that coalitions exist for a purpose. The purpose in this instance is to eliminate terrorism— with the cooperation of Islamic states if possible, but without their cooperation if necessary. Maintaining consensus at the price of inaction (a Colin Powell specialty) would be pointless.

Military operations against radical Islam have limitations of a different kind. Bin Laden's most dangerous training camps aren't in the Afghan hills where terrorists learn to shoot, but in certain *madrassas*, religious schools, in Pakistan and elsewhere, where terrorists learn to hate. Unlike training camps, *madrassas* can't be targeted by surgical air strikes.

Many commentators pointed out since September 11 that Islam stands for peace and mercy. This is true, but it's rather meaningless. All major religions stand for peace and mercy, which never stopped any major religion from having periods in which some (or most) of its followers acted in bellicose and merciless ways. Christianity stands for turning the other cheek, but this didn't prevent Christian rulers from launching nine crusades between the eleventh and thirteenth centuries to wrest the Holy Land from Islam.

In our days it's Islam that has been influenced by a militant and crusading spirit. It doesn't affect the whole Islamic world, and there's little doubt that jihad is partly a struggle within Islam itself. Still, the terrorists who launched the attack on America "reflect the mood in their home countries more than we might think," as Thomas L. Friedman remarked in the *New York Times*. Opinions may vary as to why this is so, but closing one's eyes to it is of no assistance.

As Princeton scholar Bernard Lewis, a sympathetic student of Islam, put it in an essay in 1990, "Islam has brought comfort and peace of mind to countless millions of men and women. It has given dignity and meaning to drab and impoverished lives. It has taught people of different races to live in brotherhood and people of different creeds to live side by side in reasonable tolerance.... But Islam, like other religions, has also known periods when it inspired in some of its followers a mood of hatred and violence. It is our misfortune that part, though by no means all or even most, of the Muslim world is now going through such a period, and that much, though again not all, of that hatred is directed against us."

It's essential to remember that 99.9 per cent of Muslims and Arabs aren't terrorists. But a parallel truth is that 100 per cent of the terrorists who currently threaten us are Muslims and/or Arabs. President Bush spoke of the need to "smoke terrorists out of their caves." The trouble is, the terrorists' caves aren't all in Afghanistan. Some are in New Jersey and

Florida. Others, no doubt, are in Ontario or Quebec. Much as we dislike ethnic or religious profiling for self-evident reasons, we can't disregard the fact that the current crop of terrorists recruit their members from specific religious and ethnic groups, and use their communities for camouflage.

Two hijackers lived in Paterson, N.J., whose Muslim community amounts to a large percentage of the town's population. The terrorists didn't move there in hope of assistance from their fellow Muslims—there's no evidence they sought or received any—but simply to blend into the background. There's renewed talk today about the importance of infiltrating terrorist organizations, but given the multicultural reality of Western societies, it's easier for terrorists to infiltrate, say, sky marshal programs in the West than for Western security to infiltrate terrorist cells in the Middle East.

This isn't a cause for vigilantism, only for vigilance. Muslims stretched a banner across the main street of Paterson this week, condemning the terrorists. The community and their leaders understood that with thousands buried under the rubble in New York, including many Muslims, the answer for Muslim or Arab-Americans wasn't to air their grievances, but to assert their loyalty.

The bodies of three thousand Americans lie mixed with cement dust in lower Manhattan. Some people may be tempted to turn the Muslim mobs who cheered the devastation, from Cairo to Karachi, into a similar substance. It could be achieved more easily than hunting down terrorists:

It's simpler to set fire to a haystack than to look for a needle in it. It's to the credit of Western civilization that this option is not even being contemplated.

ISLAM HIJACKED

CanWest News Service, October 16, 2001

"Islam, the religion of more than a billion believers, has been hijacked," wrote Martin Kramer, editor of *Middle East Quarterly*, in the *National Review* last month.

"Islamic radicals...mean to hijack Islam itself and to destroy thirteen centuries of Islamic civilization," offered Cleveland law professor David F. Forte, Education Affairs fellow of the Heritage Foundation.

Many commentators have talked recently about extremists and fundamentalists "hijacking" Islam. Their remarks imply that there's a genuine Islam, a pacific and benign mainstream, different from the malignant and militant fundamentalism of bin Laden and his al Qaeda network.

I'm not proposing to dispute this, only to suggest that it may not matter much. If the hijacking of Islam is successful—and there are signs showing that it may be—the nature of Islam will reflect the nature of the hijackers.

The metaphor of hijacking illustrates the point well. American Airlines Flight 11 was a pacific and benign conveyance when it departed Boston's Logan airport on

September 11, 2001. But no matter how harmless at takeoff, once it was hijacked it became a deadly threat.

George W. Bush, Tony Blair, Jean Chrétien, and other Western leaders have come close to falling over each other in their eagerness to explain that this isn't a clash of civilizations, or a war between Islam and the rest of the world. Osama bin Laden, for his part, insists just as adamantly that it is.

"These events have divided the whole world into two sides. The side of believers and the side of infidels, may God keep you away from them," bin Laden told the viewers of the Arabic news network Aljazeera. "Every Muslim has to rush to make his religion victorious."

It's not enough for Western politicians and pundits to protest that al Qaeda's leader doesn't speak for Islam. Statements refuting bin Laden would have to come from the heavy hitters of the Islamic world, and they would have to sound just as unequivocal as the chieftain of terror. It's ayatollahs like Iran's Khamenei, national leaders like Egypt's Hosni Mubarak, and kings like Jordan's Abdullah II (a forty-third generation direct descendant of the prophet Muhammad) who are in a position stop bin Laden's attempt to hijack Islam.

Unfortunately, the great leaders of the Islamic world are conspicuous by their absence from popular forums such as Aljazeera, the "Arab CNN," that commands some thirty-five million viewers. ("All this noise from this matchbox?"

President Mubarak asked disdainfully after a visit to Aljazeera's studios.) And it's not just Aljazeera; most leaders have shown little inclination so far to refute bin Laden and his followers on any Arab-language outlet.

When President Mubarak or King Abdullah demur from a clash of civilizations, when they echo the soothing words of President Bush or Prime Minister Blair, they do so in speeches or interviews designed for Western audiences. When King Abdullah appears on the *Larry King* show, any suggestion that the world is divided between believers and infidels (may God keep you away from them) seems far away. But once the *Larry King* show is over, there's mainly silence from the Hashemite kingdom. We hear no ringing statements from Muhammad's direct descendant to anathematize al Qaeda and its message.

It's all very well for President Bush—the man bin Laden calls "the head of infidels worldwide"—to tell Muslim believers that the war is waged only against terrorism, not Islam. It's necessary for Bush and other Western leaders to say so, but it's not sufficient. The message ought to come with equal force from the *ummah* of Islam, the teachers, the learned men, the role models, the community leaders.

Hard as the West tries, it alone can't distinguish al Qaeda from Islam. The Islamic world needs to distinguish itself. ("It is the militants who are...hijacking Islam," remarked the Egyptian art historian Professor Nasr Abu Zayd, but such voices are few and far between.)

Some Muslim leaders and scholars may be reluctant to speak out because they feel equivocal about the issues; some may be reluctant because they worry about the reaction of "the Arab street." Either way, their silence leaves bin Laden the dominant voice.

"We hope that these brothers [the terrorists] will be the first martyrs in the battle of Islam in this era against the new Jewish and Christian crusader campaign that is led by the Chief Crusader Bush under the banner of the cross," bin Laden proclaims. We hear, as yet, no clear reply to him from the House of Islam.

APPEASING THE ARAB STREET

National Post, October 23, 2001

Something has gone askew in the war against terrorism. The cliché that nothing would be the same after September 11 is gradually giving way to the uneasy observation that, once again, the French may have it right: The more things change, the more they remain the same.

Among the many signs, the most incongruous is Washington's concern over the sensitivities of our virtually non-existent Muslim coalition. It seems that while Muslims and Arabs object to terrorism in the abstract, they feel that particular terrorists should be left alone. So, having issued a clarion call for a global war against terrorism, U.S. president

George W. Bush and Secretary of State Colin Powell are doing their best to restrain Israel and India from retaliating against Muslim terrorists who are attacking them.

The president and his secretary urge restraint to avoid upsetting the Arab and Muslim "street," so it won't interfere with U.S. efforts to retaliate against the terrorists attacking America. It seems the Bush team wants to pursue America's war in peace. The trouble is, their feckless effort at *realpolitik* makes America seem perfidious rather than sophisticated.

While America has been launching its war on terror, the terrorists have been going to town. In Israel last week the minister of tourism, Rehavam Ze'evi, was assassinated by the Popular Front for the Liberation of Palestine. Earlier this month a suicide bomber killed forty people in Kashmir, including several legislators, in an attack on the state parliament.

"India's policymakers and major newspapers alike are seething over what they regard as the blatant hypocrisy of the United States pursuing its own self-proclaimed 'crusade against terror' to topple bin Laden's protectors, the Taliban government of Afghanistan, while it seeks to prevent India from retaliating against terrorist attacks in Kashmir," commented UPI news analyst Marty Sieff.

The problem goes beyond hypocrisy. Its worst effect is that in a vain effort to appease enemies (e.g., the Arab street), it hurts actual or potential friends. It suggests that the feelings of terrorism's apologists, from Pakistan to the Palestinian territories, take precedence over the feelings of terrorism's victims.

From the beginning, Western attempts to draw a distinction between Islamist terrorists and Islam resulted in a lopsided effort. The voices purporting to speak for Islam were largely restricted to Osama bin Laden on one side, and Western leaders on the other. Bin Laden kept saying that this was a clash between Islam and the infidels, while Western leaders, from President Bush to Canada's Jean Chrétien and Britain's Tony Blair, maintained that it wasn't.

The actual leaders of Islam remained curiously quiet. Aside from some obligatory condemnation of terrorism— usually coupled with an admonition that the West should give more support to Muslim countries and less to Israel— they said little. We rarely heard Muslims in the West pledging loyalty to the countries in which they lived, but much from President Bush and other Western heads of state announcing their loyalty to their countries' Muslim residents. In fact, our leaders made such a fuss that a Martian landing on Earth on September 12 might have thought that what happened in New York and Washington the day before wasn't Muslim terrorists massacring three thousand Americans, but American terrorists massacring three thousand Muslims.

Now the war is on, but in another illustration of Western uncertainty comes the possibility of America suspending hostilities during the Muslim holiday of Ramadan. It's unlikely to happen, but even raising the question is revealing. If a war is worth fighting, it's worth fighting over Ramadan (or Christmas, for that matter). As for Muslims being sensitive about Ramadan, as Pakistan's General Pervez Musharraf has suggested, too bad. Americans are sensitive about the three thousand fellow Americans lying in Manhattan mixed with cement dust.

Or they ought to be. One lesson of Vietnam was that a nation should never fight its wars half-heartedly. In free countries, citizens have to buy into a war, of course, before it can be waged. "If you can't sell it, don't fight it" was Vietnam's lesson for democratic leaders.

Today, with President Bush having a 90 per cent approval rating, this isn't the problem. The president never had to sell the war; the terrorists did it for him on September 11. The war might become a problem only if Mr. Bush fails to get on with it.

If the president's team gets bogged down in coalition building so much it loses sight of the purpose for which the coalition is being built; if it spends so much time reassuring America's enemies that it risks injuring or losing America's friends; if in its eagerness to maintain liberal illusions, including illusions about Islam, it ignores realities, it may make the Vietnam experience a repeat performance. Only the stakes are higher this time. The killing fields have come to Manhattan.

MEASURED TO A FAULT

CanWest News Service, October 31, 2001

The West has been pulling its punches. Ever since the main terrorist attacks of September 11, the response of the United States and its allies has been measured. Possibly it has been measured to a fault.

Almost before doing anything else, Western governments have declared that Islam is tolerant and peaceful; that the war against terror should in no way be construed as a war against Islam. To reduce any possible backlash, Western leaders have been going out of their way to ensure people won't look askance at Muslims in Western countries.

One of the first things U.S. president George W. Bush did was to visit an American mosque after Muslim terrorists killed over three thousand Americans. It was a fine gesture, but it illustrated the temper of the times. Franklin D. Roosevelt might not have chosen a visit to a Shinto shrine as one of his first engagements after Pearl Harbor.

The West didn't rush to war. It waited more than two weeks for the Afghan Taliban to surrender Osama bin Laden and his lieutenants. The bombing in Afghanistan, when it came, targeted civilians only for dropping food rations. The Taliban has been using civilian populations and infrastructure to shield military assets; the West has been trying to minimize collateral damage.

Western governments made a point of building a coalition against terrorism with Muslim countries—including countries that harboured, organized, or kept funding bin Laden's al Qaeda and similar groups, from Iran to Pakistan to Saudi Arabia. To keep these countries on side, the U.S. pressured India and Israel to exercise restraint when responding to Muslim or Arab terrorism in Kashmir and the Palestinian territories.

To cater to the sensitivities of its reluctant Muslim allies even more, the West has restrained its own war effort. The U.S. has been slow to bomb Taliban troop concentrations so as not to open up a way for the Northern Alliance, the Taliban's opponents in Afghanistan, whose entry into Kabul, the capital, would upset the Pakistanis.

The Western mantra has been coalition über alles. For the sake of coalition building, Canada's foreign minister, John Manley, has submitted this week to a lecture by Iran's foreign minister, Kamal Kharrazi, on how to fight terrorism.

Kharrazi's view is that "you have to first understand the psychological, ideological and historical factors that lead to such acts." Okay; and then what? "When the violence against Palestinians ends and four million refugees are allowed to return to their own land," Kharrazi offers, "there will be grounds for peace." In other words, the way to combat bin Laden is to accept his conditions.

Whether the West's measured response is wise or unwise may be debatable. What isn't debatable is that the Arab "street" doesn't hand out any Brownie points for it. On the contrary: the Arab street views what it regards as the West's irresolution with contempt.

In the *New York Daily News* Zev Chafets lists some of the Arab street's scornful questions: "Why would a genuine superpower, with the world's greatest economy and arsenal, need the permission and help of a so-called coalition to act against its enemies? Who, besides a coward, fears to go to war alone? Why does Secretary of State Powell claim he doesn't know if Hamas and Hezbollah are terrorists? We spit in the Americans' faces, and they pretend it is raining."

This begs an obvious question. Why does the West persist in measured and conciliatory responses if they lose rather than win hearts and minds in the Arab street? The answer may be in one of Voltaire's parables. I'm recounting it from memory.

The French philosopher's tale has an Indian sage sitting on the riverbank surrounded by his disciples, when he notices a scorpion struggling in the water. The wise man reaches in and rescues the drowning arthropod. The scorpion bites the hand that has saved it, then falls back into the water. The sage reaches in and saves the scorpion again. The scorpion promptly bites the sage's hand and drops into the river.

The uneasy disciples watch as the process is repeated again and again. Finally one of them asks: "O Master, every time you pull the scorpion out of the river, it bites you. Why do you keep saving it?"

"It's simple," replies the ancient man. "This animal and I are both doing what's in our nature. The scorpion can't help biting me because it's a scorpion. And I can't help saving it because I'm a sage."

A LESSON FROM THE PROFESSOR AND THE STATION MASTER

National Post, November 1, 2001

The story of the Turkish station master was told to me by the Hungarian icon, the poet George Faludy, now in his nineties.* He heard it from Rustem Vambery, the noted lawyer and diplomat, when they were both in New York at the end of World War II. The incident itself happened a long time ago, and it involved Vambery's father, Arminius, the nineteenth-century Orientalist.

Professor Arminius Vambery was a severely crippled man who had to use crutches. This didn't stop him from becoming an explorer of note, and the author of several important books on Central Asia. Though travelling was much more arduous in Vambery's time than in ours, especially in remote parts, the professor's crutches took him across the Hindu Kush, more or less to the region where American special units are currently poised to enter Afghanistan in search of

* Faludy passed away in 2006 at 95.

Osama bin Laden. Vambery's *Travels to Transoxiana*, published in 1883, still provides one of the best descriptions of the people on both shores the Amu Darya river.

Professor Vambery was a citizen of Austria-Hungary, and a specialist in Oriental languages. Current research suggests that he might have been associated with the British secret service in the "great game" of rivalry between the east and the west, famously described in Rudyard Kipling's novel *Kim*. Be that as it may, he was sufficiently sympathetic to the culture in which he had immersed himself to name his son Rustem, after the legendary dragon-slaying Persian hero. Professor Vambery liked the Orient. He both respected and understood it.

There were no private jets in those days, but VIPs often travelled by private railway carriage. Passing through Turkey as the Sultan's guest one year, the professor had his own carriage attached to the train. After the engine stopped at a small station in Anatolia, on the Asian side of the Marmaran Sea, a Turkish station master entered the carriage. He sized up Vambery with a sly glance, bowed perfunctorily, then informed the professor that, regrettably, his carriage needed to be uncoupled from the train.

Vambery was travelling with a friend. They looked at each other. "Why?" Vambery asked.

"Regulations, effendi," the station master replied with a smirk. "We need to leave your carriage behind on the siding. For a slight consideration, though, an exception can be made."

With that, he calmly held out his hand for baksheesh.

The station master was a huge brute, as it happened. His immense palm made a good target, so Vambery immediately whacked it with his crutch. Then he struggled to his feet, striking the Turk repeatedly with all his might.

The station master, who could have snapped the professor in half, didn't even try to ward off the blows. "Effendi, I didn't know, forgive me, I didn't realize..." he muttered, bowing deeply and backing off. "In your exalted case, of course, regulations don't apply..."

"Didn't you see the size of that fellow?" Vambery's friend asked, shaken, after the genuflecting giant had backed out of the car. "Weren't you afraid to hit him?"

"Of course," replied Vambery, "but this is the Orient. I would have been far more afraid not to hit him."

Vambery's assessment of what is to be feared more, firmness or appeasement, holds true in many parts of the world, not just the Orient. Except in the East it's more than a rule of thumb. It's one of the fundamentals, which Westerners, especially Americans, have trouble appreciating.

This goes beyond the classic problem of decency or compromise being mistaken for weakness. What Americans find hard to understand is that gestures of magnanimity aren't seen as such in Eastern cultures. In fact, they have the opposite effect. Stopping air attacks for Muslim religious holidays, for instance, or dropping food parcels after bombing raids, not only fail get America any Brownie points, but often aggravate resentment.

Alms alternating with bombs seem deliberately humiliating. They add insult to injury. They signal the ostentation of power. To the Oriental mind, especially, such humanitarian gestures show America's arrogance and swaggering tackiness, not its heart.

They also telegraph unease, guilt, maybe even fear.

There's a bewildered question Americans, and Westerners in general, keep asking after 9/11: "Why do they hate us so?" The question also has an unasked corollary: "Why don't they respect us more?" The answer may be that we haven't yet learned when to whack the station master and when to offer him baksheesh.

THE BIG POWERS HAVE HAD IT

National Post, November 4, 2001

Future alignments in the world may take unexpected turns. Familiar rifts—North and South, rich and poor, white and non-white—may no longer be essential fault lines. The main battle front isn't likely to be drawn between statist systems and free enterprise democracies, or the "infidel" and Islam, or the West and the rest. Though previous divisions—racial, economic, religious, and political—will remain, they'll become reduced in significance.

Chances are that the coming "clash of civilizations" won't be modernity versus medievalism, or tyrannies butting heads with free countries. Instead, it will be major powers putting minor powers in their place. It will be a clash between shakos and sheep-stealers, to borrow a nineteenth-century image.

"Shakos" meant civilized Europe. The word for the rigid, cylindrical military headgear was used rather like the word "suits" is used today. "Sheep-stealers" was the disdainful expression German chancellor Otto von Bismarck employed to describe the peoples of the Balkans. It was like "cave-dwellers," the word the Western media favours to describe not only al Qaeda and the Taliban, but the entire region between the Amu Darya and the Hindu Kush. Such words are expressions of the contempt strong, mature, vigorous, and accomplished cultures often feel for weak, immature, exhausted, or unaccomplished cultures: cultures that seem unable to feed, govern, or come to terms with themselves, or are sources of upheaval and turmoil.

Major nations scorn minor nations almost as a matter of course, but such routine derision isn't invariably coupled with hostility. Often it's combined with curiosity bordering on affection, encompassing protective and beneficial impulses. They can create big-power champions for "underdog" nations, like Lawrence of Arabia.

Hostility comes when "sheep-stealers" or "cave-dwellers" disturb the equilibrium of major powers—as the Serbs did when one of them assassinated the heir to the Habsburg throne, sparking World War I, much as Bismarck had anticipated it. Or, more recently, when another Serb, Slobodan Milosevic, tried to use brutish measures to prevent the secession of the Serbian province of Kosovo. Resentment ensues when remote and barely comprehensible tribal conflicts, whether between Pashtuns and Tajiks, or even Israelis and Palestinians, spill over into what we regard as the civilized world.

Resentment and hostility don't always result in major powers ganging up on minor ones. Usually major powers exploit the instabilities or grievances of minor entities by inciting them against rival major powers, or utilize them as buffer zones. This is what happened in many regions during the Cold War.

In the post–Cold War era, however, major power rivalries are at a relatively low ebb. There's an equilibrium— somewhat uneasy, but an equilibrium still—between the United States, Russia, China, Japan, the European Union, and India. The balance of power may be unstable and it may not last, but at present it exists. Peace isn't threatened by big-power rivalries, but by the ambitions, insecurities, jealousies, and grievances of minor nations and tribes jockeying for position around the edges of contemporary history.

As the new millennium begins, it's the appetites or gripes of Basques, Bosnians, Chechens, Hutus, Israelis, Kosovars, Kurds, Macedonians, Palestinians, Serbs, Tibetans, Tutsis, Uzbeks, Uighurs, and similar minor entities that are upsetting the tranquility of the world—along, of course, with the militant Sunni or Shiite fundamentalists of Afghanistan, Pakistan, Kashmir, Algeria, Sudan, Egypt, Saudi Arabia, and Iran. Likewise the two remaining small Marxist dictatorships in Cuba and North Korea, as well as a few Arab states in the grip of aggressive tyrants of nationalistic or quasi-Marxist rather than Islamist bent, such as Iraq, Libya, and Syria.

What these entities have in common is that they don't amount to a hill of beans economically, technologically, or culturally. A few may have mattered once, but no longer. If they ceased to exist—in some cases, if they never existed—it would make no difference to the accomplishments of mankind in art, science, technology, exploration, economy, literature, or philosophy. Even oil doesn't provide sufficient leverage for such cultures in a world of alternate technologies. Though together they may have the weight of numbers (e.g., if Islamists succeeded in "hijacking" Islam, they could array a billion Muslims against the rest of the world), taken one by one, even the largest among them, such as Pakistan, would be no military match to the major powers at present.

From the point of view of the significant powers—not only the U.S., the E.U., Russia, China, Japan, and India, but also Australia, Canada, Latin America, and South Korea—these minor and often dysfunctional countries or tribes have nothing but nuisance value. Their constructive significance is almost non-existent, yet their destructive significance is considerable. Their aspirations or laments constitute a menace to the stability of regions in which the major powers have finally achieved a precarious balance. The U.S. and the E.U. aren't looking for trouble in the Balkans or the Middle East, while China and Russia positively want to avoid it in their Muslim provinces or neighbourhoods. At present Beijing would sooner buy military technology from America, such as spare parts for its Blackhawk helicopters, than continue playing a game of "let's annoy India" by supporting Pakistan over Kashmir—especially when China has problems with its own Muslim Uighurs in the province of Xinjiang.

Though most Uighurs, as a recent *Washington Post* editorial rightly points out, "are secular, nationalist and pro-democracy," some have been touched by bin Laden's spirit. "In recent years some militants have carried out bombings and assassinations of Chinese officials, and a few hundred have traveled to Afghanistan or Pakistan for military or religious training," notes the *Washington Post*. In this climate, annoying India or even annexing Taiwan takes second place. China no more needs Uighurs crashing hijacked jets into the Forbidden City than the U.S. needed Arab hijackers crashing into the World Trade Center.

And hijackers are the least of it. By now, some of Bismarck's sheep-stealers—notably Iraq, North Korea, and Pakistan—have developed, or are in the process of developing, weapons of mass destruction. It's obvious that an "Islamic bomb" in the hands of a Saddam Hussein* or an

---

* Saddam Hussein was executed in 2006.

Osama bin Laden would be an intolerable threat to life on earth. It's equally obvious that the major powers know it.

The much vaunted "root causes" scarcely come into play at this stage. It no longer matters if some marginal countries resent major powers for valid reasons, such as having been repressed, exploited, or betrayed by them, or for unworthy reasons, such as feelings of inferiority, spite, and envy. In either case, what major powers feel for marginal groups is the hostility of urban commuters for obnoxious panhandlers wielding squeegees.

The big powers have had it. If during the Cold War the U.S. backed Israel against the Soviet Union, while Soviet Russia backed the Palestinians against the U.S., in today's climate both the U.S. and Russia prefer to back each other against troublesome Jews and Muslims alike. Russian prime minister Vladimir Putin has a million soldiers near the Afghan border, and seems poised to make a deal with President Bush.

Some minor nations are beginning to realize that they've been pushing the envelope. This year the Serbs have surrendered their national leader, Milosevic, to the International War Crimes Tribunal in The Hague. Iran seems ready to do something similar (or worse) to its ayatollahs.

This may be prudent, because the next coalition to emerge is likely to be the world's shakos against the world's sheep-stealers. Yes, the West may be uneasy with some measures Russia is liable to employ against the

Chechens, or China against the Uighurs, but it will keep its unease to itself.

WAR IS A SOLILOQUY

CanWest News Service, November 7, 2001

Ever since the day Islamist terrorists killed three thousand Americans, every Western leader has solemnly declared that Islam isn't the enemy. Tactical or heartfelt, such declarations seem rather futile. If Islam comes to regard the West as its enemy, it no longer matters how the West regards Islam.

It takes two to tango, but only one to mug. Osama bin Laden and company have made up their minds that there's a clash between the faithful and the "unbelievers." ("Under no circumstances should we forget this enmity between us and the infidels. For the enmity is based on creed," explains bin Laden in his latest video, released on November 3.) If the militants can get a sufficient number of Muslims to agree with them, the clash will come, whether we like it or not.

Peace is a dialogue; war is a soliloquy. The non-Islamic world may cling to the illusion that Islam is tolerant and peaceful—Islam may *be* tolerant and peaceful, for that matter—but if Islam cannot, or will not, prevent fanatics acting in its name from terrorizing the non-Islamic world, sooner or later the non-Islamic world will find itself at war with Islam. Once a civilization is usurped by people who consider themselves at war with another civilization, there will be a clash of civilizations. It is as simple as that.

Another simple fact is that the militants of Islam have no way of carrying a war to the Western nations they consider their enemies, except through Arabs and Muslims who live in Western countries as students, visitors, refugees, or citizens. Islam has no military means to project its power upon the West. Al Qaeda has no armies, navies, air forces, or long-range missiles sufficient to penetrate Western perimeters. Its only weapons are Arab and/or Muslim residents in Western countries.

We've nothing to fear from an Islamist enemy outside our borders. Our danger comes from Arabs/Muslims who dwell among us. Yet the West spends infinitely more on tanks, attack helicopters, and aircraft carriers than on counterintelligence, internal security, and immigration control.

Except Canada, one should add. Canada spends little on either.

Obviously, most Muslims and/or Arabs who live in Western countries aren't terrorists. Even sympathizers and apologists are probably a minority. But the needs of terrorism are frugal. In this kind of warfare, nineteen suicidal attackers, armed with box cutters, can down four airliners, demolish two of the world's largest structures, damage the Pentagon, cause thousands of American casualties, and send the economy into a tailspin. If only one out of a hundred Muslims in America sympathizes with al Qaeda, and only one out of a thousand sympathizers is ready to commit a terrorist act, we have enough Islamist terrorists among our neighbours for three more September 11s.

What can we do about it? To begin with, we can face it. Discarding illusions may not be a sufficient strategy against terrorism, but it's a necessary first step.

We need not repeat the mistakes of sixty years ago when we interned loyal Americans and Canadians just because of their Japanese ancestry. But if sixty years ago we took needless steps against loyal residents and citizens, today we're reluctant to take needful steps against openly disloyal ones.

Take Britain, where some young Muslims have volunteered to fight for the Taliban and against their own country. Two volunteers, Afzal Munir and Aftab Manzoor, both twenty-five, from Luton, Bedfordshire, as well as a third man from Crawley, West Sussex, were reportedly killed last week in Kabul, Afghanistan, during the American bombing.

Muslim communities have expressed sympathy for the volunteers. The BBC has quoted Ajmol Masroor of the Islamic Society of Britain saying that "with the current policy of attacking innocent Afghanis, I think we're alienating a vast majority of second generation Muslims." Akbar Khan, another community leader, has observed that "There's a lot of unhappiness among Muslims in Luton and the rest of the country about the attitude of the West."

The response of Britain's defence secretary, Geoff Hoon, has been to wag a disapproving finger at young men who volunteer to aid the enemy in wartime. "I hope that anyone who is contemplating going to Afghanistan does think very carefully about the consequences," he said.

Not a very strong reaction against treason. As Osama bin Laden remarked in his latest video, "a person who is misguided by God can never be guided by anyone." One wonders if he had the God of liberalism in mind.

ON PRE-EMPTIVE WAR
National Post, November 11, 2001

Last week Osama bin Laden told Pakistani journalist Hamid Mir that he had nuclear weapons. This was almost certainly a lie. However, al Qaeda's leader would no doubt like to have nuclear weapons, which raises a question. What justifies pre-emptive action?

To illustrate, probably no month passes without a police officer being investigated somewhere for reckless use of a firearm. The fact situation is often the same. A fleeing or resisting suspect appears to reach for what the officer thinks is a gun, to which the officer responds by shooting first.

At the same time probably no month passes without a police officer being shot. It often happens because the officer chooses not to fire pre-emptively, but waits until the fleeing or resisting suspect points a weapon.

This, in a nutshell, is the problem with pre-emptive action. By definition, pre-emptive action is always "too early." If it's not too early, it isn't pre-emptive, and if it's not pre-emptive, it's often too late.

The dilemma becomes infinitely greater when it doesn't involve just police officers and guns, but nations and nuclear weapons. This is the dilemma facing U.S. president George W. Bush's administration today.

In a speech delivered by satellite to the Warsaw meeting of East European leaders last week, the President raised the spectre of bin Laden's al Qaeda network going after nuclear weapons. Mr. Bush's reference wasn't merely rhetorical; he didn't just add the word "nuclear" to the chemical and biological weapons of mass destruction bin Laden (or Iraq's Saddam Hussein) is known to be going after. Though Mr. Bush spoke before bin Laden made his claim, the president's reference was quite specific.

Pakistan has nuclear weapons. While General Pervez Musharraf's government is currently America's ally (sort of) in the war against terrorism, Pakistan itself was instrumental in setting up the Taliban regime in Afghanistan. There's a substantial and militant minority in Pakistan—mainly among the general population, but also in the governing elite, such as the powerful Inter-Service Intelligence or ISI—that supports the Taliban. The Taliban, of course, hosts and protects al Qaeda.

General Musharraf's government is by no means secure. If it were to be toppled, there's at least a possibility that bin Laden might actually gain access to nuclear weapons. (According to the *Daily Telegraph*, two Pakistani nuclear scientists admitted yesterday having met bin Laden earlier this year, and Pakistan moved its nuclear weapons "to ensure their safety in the event of an Islamic coup.") The scenario, though not likely, has something like a 5 per cent probability. A small chance—but with colossal consequences.

No responsible government would put up with a 5 per cent chance of a comparable catastrophe in any area of law enforcement or public hygiene. The authorities would unquestionably take the position than an ounce of pre-emption is worth a pound of cure.

But what would "pre-emption" entail in such a case? Nothing very nice. On a minor scale, consider Waco. Though the FBI may have stormed David Koresh's compound partly as an expression of administrative vengeance, primarily they did so to pre-empt a fanatical cult from harming others with their arsenal of illegal firearms. In spite of this, the ensuing mayhem, particularly the fiery deaths of children, rightly shocked the conscience of a nation.

Obviously the mayhem at Waco would be a Boy Scout jamboree compared to the results of a pre-emptive incursion (let alone a pre-emptive nuclear strike) on a country. How would the mere possession of nuclear capability justify such an attack?

Yet when the authorities pleaded after Waco that they had a duty to force their way into Koresh's compound because of the threat Koresh and his armed disciples represented to the larger community, the courts agreed. By this standard, it would be hard to argue that weapons of mass destruction in the hands of countries like Pakistan or Iraq represent anything less than a grievous threat to the entire world.

Some might counter that just raising the question in these terms amounts to Western arrogance. After all, no one loses any sleep over, say, France's nuclear capabilities. If France can have weapons of mass destruction without the world feeling endangered, why should Pakistan, or even Iraq, be judged by a different yardstick? What's wrong with a "Muslim bomb"? If the West can possess nuclear weapons, why can't Islam?

Someone like Italian prime minister Silvio Berlusconi might blurt out in reply (as he did in September) that it's because the West is more civilized than Islam—and then quickly apologize for the remark. Yet, in truth, if France's bomb never inspired anyone to pre-emptive action, the reason was that France's neighbours felt safe betting their lives on France a) being able to keep its nuclear arsenal from falling into unauthorized hands, and b) not using nuclear weapons except in self-defence, and as a last resort.

In other words, France's neighbours were willing to bet on France being both stable and civilized. Would Pakistan's or Iraq's neighbours bet their lives on the same assumptions?

A TALE OF TWO MALIGNANCIES
National Post, November 26, 2001

The state's response to terrorism after September 11 came in three varieties. In this respect there was little difference between Canada, the United Kingdom, and the United States. Writing in the *Daily Telegraph* last week, Barbara Amiel described the three as "Safe Rules," "Mixed Rules," and "Dead Wrong."

Amiel's "Safe Rules" denoted changes in law or governmental authority designed to hinder terrorists without curtailing the rights and freedoms of ordinary citizens (e.g., facilities working with toxins now had to furnish their list of employees to the authorities). "Mixed Rules" had some anti-terrorist utility, but were also designed for unrelated governmental purposes, along with procedures that arguably restricted the freedom or privacy of citizens more than necessary (e.g., intrusive regulations concerning overseas business transactions). "Dead Wrong" were enhancements of state authority that affected terrorism only marginally if at all, and were mainly designed to extend the government's bureaucratic powers, enforce its socio-political agendas, and reduce its accountability (e.g., new disclosure rules).

Such power-grab was no more palatable for being expected. "All governments, be they elected or imposed, strive ceaselessly to maximize their power," as the *Daily Telegraph*'s Robert Harris put it last week, "and never is this more easily done than during wartime." After September 11 the state responded by doing what it does best, which is to spread like a cancer.

But the analogy also works in reverse. While terrorism triggers a malignant metastasis by the state, terrorism itself is a malignancy. Terror kills when left untreated; the problem is, the radical surgery or intensive chemotherapy of anti-terrorism can kill the patient (i.e., a free society), almost as easily.

Depending on temperament and ideology, some people tend to minimize the first problem, and some minimize the second.

Just as anti-terrorist measures come in three varieties, so do most objections to them. Critics of Canada's Bill C-36— or the even more sweeping Public Safety Act, introduced last week under the guise of housekeeping legislation—consist of a) genuine civil libertarians, b) civil libertarians with side agendas, such as being soft on drugs or radical dissent, and c) apologists for terrorism.

In any debate about civil liberties, false notes abound. Some commentators on the Palestinian side of the Middle East conflict try to obscure the threat of militant Islam whose fifth columns of theo-fascist storm troopers have infiltrated Western democracies—as have other separatist or anarchical movements, from the Tamil Tigers to the ruffians of CLAC (la Convergence des luttes Anticapitalistes). But no amount of sympathy for "root causes" can alter the fact that these movements use intimidation and violence to bolster their political aims. Anti-poverty or anti-globalist protesters may be merely disruptive, but the militants of tribal separatism or theocracy, whether of the Basque, Tamil, Sikh, or Islamist variety, have frequently been murderous.

But while terrorism is a menace, some remedies are perfidious themselves or seem totally beside the point. How would stiffer penalties for air rage reduce the threat of September 11? Or barring citizens from seeking compensation if they're injured by being evicted from some newly designed "military security zone"? On the other hand, why doesn't the Public Safety Act provide for air marshals, a measure that might actually counter a terrorist threat?

Arguably more could be done to safeguard Canada from terrorists by a fundamental restructuring of the Immigration and Refugee Board (IRB) than by any new legislation. The majority of the IRB's current political appointees come from the immigration and refugee lobby. While most probably wouldn't endorse the practice of crashing airplanes into office buildings, many seem to believe that "one man's terrorist is another man's freedom fighter."

At least this is my guess, bolstered by such bits as a line in a recent column by the *Toronto Star*'s Haroon Siddiqui. "Tell us, please, how you propose to resolve the dilemma over one person's terrorist being another's liberation fighter," wrote Mr. Siddiqui in an open letter to Justice Minister Anne McLellan on November 8, questioning Bill C-36. As it happens,

Yasmeen Siddiqui, Mr. Siddiqui's wife, is a member of the IRB. If Mr. Siddiqui's inability to tell a terrorist from a freedom fighter extends to other members of his family, along with like-minded colleagues and friends, it would explain some of the IRB's decisions. (A hint for Mr. Siddiqui: if someone flies an airliner into a high-rise or blows up a disco filled with teenagers, for any reason, it's safe to assume he's a terrorist.)

But the problem goes beyond granting bogus refugee claims, whether to actual terrorists or to spurious applicants. Even when refugee claims are rejected, Canada has failed to enforce an unknown number of deportation orders. We're just beginning to realize that Islamist activists allegedly linked to Osama bin Laden, such as Said Atmani or Samir Ait Mohamed, have been able to operate in this country for years. Worse, as Christie Blatchford reported last week, no one seems to know if some current illegals, such as Sahrif Abouhalima, whose brother Mahmud was convicted in the U.S. in relation to the World Trade Center bombing of 1993, are still in the country or not.

There's no end to what we don't know. As Kenneth Whyte pointed out in an editorial last week, we don't know "the severity, persistence and sweep" of terrorist operations in Canada. We don't know "the degree to which we contribute, however unintentionally, to the sum of misery and bloodshed beyond our borders."

If, instead of trying to grab new powers, governments used their existing powers more efficiently, the terrorist threat might be reduced, or at least become clearer. Unfortunately, this is probably against the nature of governments. As for left-lib critics, if they refrained from engaging in discussion about civil liberties until they learn how to tell terrorists from freedom fighters, it would elevate the tone of the debate. Unfortunately, this is probably against the nature of left-lib critics.

GOING TO WAR FOR MAKEUP

CanWest News Service, November 28, 2001

Toronto *Globe and Mail* columnist Margaret Wente is concerned that the Northern Alliance, now poised to take power in Afghanistan, may not treat women much better than the Taliban did. Ditto for some other rulers in the Middle East.

Ms. Wente writes that U.S. president George W. Bush's job of nation building won't be done "until women in Saudi Arabia are allowed to drive and women in Kuwait are allowed to vote. It won't be done until women who don't cover up are freed from beatings by the religious police.... The West cannot tolerate terrorists against women, or those who harbour them."

I wonder. It seems to me the only thing the West cannot tolerate is having its airplanes, buildings, and citizens blown up.

What the West cannot tolerate is being attacked. If attacked, it has to respond in kind. The West cannot tolerate what others do to it. However, the West not only can, but arguably should, tolerate what others do to themselves. If the West doesn't tolerate other societies arranging their affairs in their own way, the West reverts to being an imperialist power.

Perhaps there's something to be said for being an imperialist power and a civilizing influence in the world, except this isn't the usual view of people who think of themselves as "progressives" and "liberals." Normally, such people are the first to detect and decry any manifestation of what they call "cultural imperialism." It's amusing, actually, how quickly liberals lose their abhorrence of cultural imperialism when it comes to one of their own agendas.

One doesn't have to be a feminist, of course, to consider women being beaten by police for failing to cover up offensive, but one may have to be a non-Afghan. I find Saudi women not being allowed to drive offensive, too, only a) I'm not a Saudi, and b) I'm not convinced that I'm entitled to interfere in everything I consider offensive.

Buildings destroyed in Manhattan are very much a matter for President Bush, but Saudi women driving is only a matter for Saudi men and women. I wouldn't hesitate sending the Marines against every regime in the Middle East that stockpiles weapons of mass destruction, but I don't think I'd go to war to enable Saudi women to drive. Much as I favour the women of Kuwait to be fully franchised, or the women of Afghanistan to be able to wear makeup whenever they please, I wouldn't fire a single Cruise missile, let alone put a single Western soldier in harm's way for it.

I agree with Ms. Wente that the militants of Islam terrorize women, at least according to our lights, but this is something for Islam to resolve. Imposing our values on another civilization in a matter of gender roles is cultural imperialism of the most self-evident kind. Liberals would take this for granted if it were a question of any other Western value, from individual liberty to the rule of law— but for the sake of women driving or wearing makeup they seem ready to make war on the entire Middle East. It certainly shows where liberal priorities are these days.

It's liberal priorities, by the way, that upset the opponents of modernity in the Middle East as much as America's support for Israel. The militants of Islam feel slighted by the sight of women driving or running around with their faces painted no less than by the existence of what they call the Zionist entity. Needless to say, this doesn't oblige the West to change its stance on either women or Israel. But it's useful to remember how much Islamists resent the West for its secular and liberal culture even without reference to the Palestinian conflict.

Someone may ask if it would have been "cultural imperialism" for the West to go to war with Hitler for persecuting Germany's Jews. It's a moot point, because we didn't go to war with Nazi Germany for that reason. We didn't declare war even when Hitler annexed Austria or marched into Czechoslovakia. The war came only when Hitler attacked Poland, giving the West no choice.

Perhaps it's lucky that ideological fanatics tend to overplay their hand. After taking over and terrorizing their own cultures, sooner or later they attack Poland—or Manhattan. Then the West can legitimately pull out its big guns and do all the things it couldn't do while the evil-doers merely attacked Jewish or female or dissident members of their own civilizations.

BRING ME A CUP OF TEA

National Post, December 13, 2001

Militant Islam is feeling its oats. Yesterday a suicide squad invaded India's parliament buildings and assassinated seven people before dying themselves. One terrorist met his maker when he detonated explosives strapped to his body, and the other four expired in a gun battle with the police.

No one claimed immediate responsibility, but the assumption that the terrorists were Islamists and the issue, Kashmir, is taken for granted. "Where is the doubt? What is there to prove?" asked Raghubir Singh, a member of the ruling Bharatiya Janata Party, as many of India's parliamentarians called for emulating America's action in Afghanistan.

India's dispute with its minorities isn't restricted to Muslims over Kashmir, though, nor is Islam the only movement producing suicide bombers. Prime Minister Indira Gandhi was assassinated by Sikh separatists in 1984, and her son, Rajiv Gandhi, was killed by a Tamil suicide bomber while serving as prime minister in 1991.

Ever since becoming independent in 1947, India has played an ambivalent role vis-à-vis terrorism as well as the independence of other people. Under Jawaharlal Nehru and his daughter, Indira Gandhi, India rivalled Canada in its resolve to be the world's leading fence sitter. During the Cold War, India, even more than Canada, hoped to achieve moral standing by observing strict neutrality between good and evil (i.e., democracy and tyranny). In the 1990s, it firmly condemned terrorism, provided it was directed against India, while being supportive, or at least equivocal, about terrorism directed against others, notably Israel.

As recently as December 5, India's minister of external affairs, Shri Jaswant Singh, stated, "We are deeply concerned at the recent escalation of violence in [West Asia]. The terrorist attacks have led to large number of casualties and injuries to very many innocent people. We condemn such acts." Then, in the same speech, Mr. Singh announced that "the Government of India is observing today the International Day of Solidarity with the Palestinian People," adding that "[w]e sincerely hope that nothing will be done to undermine President Arafat and Palestinian National

Authority as the alternatives are fraught with dangers having serious implications for regional peace and security."

In other words, as recently as a week ago Prime Minister Atal Behari Vajpayee's government saw nothing incongruous about supporting the PNA, Yasser Arafat's safe haven for the suicide bombers of Hamas, while indignantly denouncing Pakistan's sponsorship of Kashmiri militancy. After yesterday's attack, however, Indian government spokesmen sounded positively Bush-like. "We will liquidate the terrorists and their sponsors whoever they are, wherever they are," announced Home Minister L.K. Advani.

The word "wherever" in this context translates to "Pakistan." Understanding this, Pakistani president Pervez Musharraf wasted no time in condemning the terrorists and sending a message of sympathy to Prime Minister Vajpayee. Though General Musharraf sounded a bit like Chairman Arafat on TV giving blood after the bombing of World Trade Center, his impulse was a shade more genuine. Unlike the Palestinian chairman, General Musharraf isn't merely auditioning for the role of Tartuffe, Molière's classic hypocrite. While Mr. Arafat has been using the terrorists of Hamas as the cat's paw for his own policy aims, General Musharraf is actually battling Islamist militants within Pakistan.

The real problem isn't suicide bombers in this case, but nuclear weapons. Nuclear weapons are scary things, no matter who controls them, but in the hands of excitable chaps they're scary beyond measure. I wouldn't call the inhabitants of the Indian subcontinent "excitable," by the way, if there were a politically correct word of equal accuracy to describe them, but I can't think of any. Individual Indians and Pakistanis may be no more excitable than other people, but as cultures, they certainly have been.

Looking at India and Pakistan facing each other over Kashmir, each armed with nuclear weapons, what can the world wish for? I'm reminded of a joke that was current about half a century ago.

World War II is ending in 1945—the joke goes—as Soviet leader J.V. Stalin enters the celestial café, accompanied by U.S. President Harry Truman and British Prime Minister Winston Churchill. The heavenly waiter approaches to take their order.

"Tell you what," says Stalin. "Since we're in heaven, bring me an atomic bomb large enough to devastate half of America."

"Lemme see that menu," Truman says. "Okay, I'll have your jumbo thermonuclear device that can take out the entire Soviet Union."

The waiter jots down the orders, then turns to Churchill.

"Hmm," says the prime minister. "I think you should serve these two gentlemen first, then bring me a cup of tea."

2002

WHO HAS THE STRONGER HORSE?

CanWest News Service, January 1, 2002

In his notorious dinner conversation videotaped in November, Osama bin Laden remarked at one point that "when people see a strong horse and a weak horse, by nature, they will like the strong horse." Presumably he meant that the terrorist action of September 11 demonstrated the superior strength of militant Islam. He proudly recounted that "in Holland, at one of the [Islamic] centers, the number of people who accepted Islam during the days that followed the operations were more than the people who accepted Islam in the last eleven years."

It's interesting that people with the greatest faith in force often have the poorest ability to measure it. The late Adolf Hitler and bin Laden are both cases in point, though they were preceded by Napoleon. The Corsican adventurer also proclaimed that "God is on the side of the big battalions," before proceeding to take on battalions that, in combination, were significantly bigger than the Grand Army of the French.

Bin Laden may not be wrong about people naturally preferring a strong horse to a weak horse. He's just doesn't seem to know much about horses. He resembles Hitler not only in his quest for dominance or in his hatred of Jews, but in the almost comic divergence between his mathematical theories and his ability to add up numbers.

Hitler's world view was similarly predicated on the idea that Providence favours the strong. He, too, felt that "might is right," not merely as a practical but as a moral proposition, expressing nature's preference for the survival of the fittest. But then he proceeded to miscalculate the relative strength of Germany and her Axis partners in relation to the strength of the Atlantic Alliance in rather incongruous ways.

To believe that God is on the side of the big battalions is one thing, but to believe it, and then conclude, as Hitler did, that Germany, Italy, and Japan could triumph over the combined resources, wealth, and manpower of mankind led by Great Britain, the British Commonwealth, and the United States is quite another. That's not how the numbers add up in the racing form, which bin Laden also has a problem reading. To believe that between militant Islam and an aroused America the race would go to militant Islam, is betting on the wrong horse.

There's little doubt that America has been aroused. Here, for instance, is the text of a U.S. military radio broadcast to the Taliban forces. I can't resist quoting it in its entirety:

Attention Taliban! You are condemned. Did you know that? The instant the terrorists you support took over our planes, you sentenced yourselves to death. The Armed Forces of the United States are here to seek justice for our dead. Highly trained soldiers are coming to shut down once and for all Osama bin Laden's ring of terrorism, and the Taliban that supports them and their actions.

Our forces are armed with state-of-the-art military equipment. What are you using: obsolete and ineffective weaponry? Our helicopters will rain fire down upon your camps before you detect them on your radar. Our bombs are so accurate we can drop them right through your windows. Our infantry is trained for any climate and terrain on earth. United States' soldiers fire with superior marksmanship and are armed with superior weapons.

You have only one choice.... Surrender now and we will give you a second chance. We will let you live. If you surrender no harm will come to you. When you decide to surrender, approach United States forces with your hands in the air. Sling your weapon across your back, muzzle towards the ground. Remove your magazine and expel any rounds. Doing this is your only chance of survival.

Before September 11, such a broadcast would have been unthinkable—in fact, the very language would have sounded un-American. Actually, the language sounds rather Asiatic, which may be appropriate, considering to whom it's being addressed.

It appears that if bin Laden has succeeded in one thing, it has been to push America into an era of post-liberalism. The U.S. has begun to talk the talk of a hyper-power, and has also been walking the walk in the last three months. I don't mind the walk, but find the talk vaguely disconcerting. I hope it won't become a habit. There's no question that America has the big battalions; what's less certain, in spite of Napoleon's view, is that God is invariably on their side.

THE CRESCENT MOON IS MADE OF BLUE CHEESE
National Post, March 1, 2002

A recent Gallup poll conducted for *USA Today* brings us good news and bad news. To start with the bad news, it seems that 61 per cent of the inhabitants of such Islamic countries as Indonesia, Iran, Jordan, Kuwait, Lebanon,

Morocco, Pakistan, Saudi Arabia, and Turkey believe that Arabs weren't responsible for the attacks of September 11.

One popular theory in the Muslim world has Israel's intelligence service, the Mossad, hijacking the airliners and crashing them into the Pentagon and the World Trade Center. The story that four thousand Jews stayed away from Manhattan's twin towers on the morning of 9/11 has been circulating in the region for months.

In addition to the question about the responsibility for the 9/11 attacks, the poll queried nearly ten thousand respondents in nine Islamic countries on various related topics, such as their opinion on U.S. president George W. Bush (58 per cent unfavourable) or whether the U.S. military action in Afghanistan was morally justified (77 per cent said it was unjustified). Though revealing, these questions and answers illuminated little that wasn't already known about popular sentiment in the Muslim world.

The question about the responsibility for 9/11 (which three countries, Saudi Arabia, Jordan, and Morocco, didn't permit the Gallup researchers to ask) was in a different class. The identity of the 9/11 hijackers wasn't a matter of opinion. Here the poll didn't deal with judgment or interpretation, but with facts.

If a question about, say, the composition of the moon elicited a 61 per cent response of "blue cheese," one might doubt the rationality of the culture that produced the answer. This raises a point of irony. Centuries ago, when the

Western world was mired in the Dark Ages, it was in no small measure the rationality of Islam that influenced the Renaissance in Europe. In 1300 (the year 700 in the Muslim calendar) the West could have taken—and did take—lessons in rationality, tolerance, and enlightenment from Islam. Seven centuries later, alas, it's the rationality of Islamic culture that's seriously in doubt.

What's the good news? Look at it this way. The 61 per cent who refuse to accept that the perpetrators of September 11 were Arabs at least exhibit certain moral standards. They consider crashing civilian airliners into office buildings wrong.

It's heartening that 61 per cent of Muslims have the moral capacity to be troubled by the mass murder of office workers and airline passengers, which is why they refuse to believe that fellow Muslims had anything to do with it. Their inability to face the truth shows that they find the truth unpalatable. This is a hopeful sign. It indicates that a majority of Muslims exists on a higher moral plane than Osama bin Laden and his suicide bombers of al Qaeda, or the "martyrs" of Hamas and Hezbollah, who view indiscriminate murder with pride.

Unfortunately, the relief is momentary. The problem appears to go deeper than bin Laden's acolytes. The number of Muslims who can't accept that Arabs were responsible for 9/11 roughly coincides with the number (about 66 per cent) who believe the atrocities at the World Trade Center and the

Pentagon were morally unjustifiable. A smaller number, however, believes the opposite (i.e., that the attack was justified). This means that most of the Muslim world is split into two groups. There's a larger one that has moral reservations about 9/11 but doesn't believe Arabs were responsible for it, and a smaller one that has no moral reservations about mass murder.

It's hard to say what should trouble us more. Is it the majority's inability to face self-evident facts, or is it that a sizable minority (as high as 36 per cent, for example, in Kuwait) thinks the attacks were justified? The latter figures, if representative of the Muslim world as a whole, project between three hundred million and four hundred million human beings on this planet who think that their sense of grievance, whatever it stems from, justifies indiscriminate slaughter. It makes one rather concerned about Islamic countries that seek to build a "Muslim bomb" or similar weapons of mass destruction.

One additional point: Tuesday's Gallup poll puts into stark perspective a recent and much-discussed proposal by Saudi Arabia. This plan, as described in the *New York Times* last week, would have all Arab states in the region recognize Israel in exchange for Israel withdrawing from the Palestinian territories back to the borders that existed before the Six Day War in 1967. It's a plan Israeli foreign minister Shimon Peres reportedly called a "fascinating, interesting opportunity."

I think the proposal bears repeating slowly. Israel, it's suggested, should give up territory, buffer zones, and Jerusalem's Temple Mount in exchange for a declaration of "recognition" by Middle East countries—that is, the very countries whose inhabitants either think that September 11 was the work of the Israelis (about 60 per cent), or that crashing hijacked airliners into Lower Manhattan was justified (about 30 per cent).

If Oslo was supposed to be about "land for peace," what should one call the Saudi deal? "Land for empty promises by irrational people"? Mr. Peres may consider such a proposal a fascinating opportunity. I'd be more inclined to consider it suicidal.

MILITANT ISLAM IS NOT THERE BUT HERE

National Post, March 29, 2002

Last week Afghanistan opened its schools again to flocks of children of both sexes. The boys seemed eager and delighted; the girls even more so. The Taliban hadn't allowed girls to be educated for six years. The news clips showed moments of genuine joy, illustrating something unambiguously good that happened in the world since September 11.

Unfortunately, Afghan girls going to school and Afghan adults playing music and taking photographs are the only unambiguously positive results of the war on terrorism so far. This is because, in one important sense, the war is being fought in the wrong place.

If the West had gone to war just to liberate Afghanistan, it would have achieved its aim. But the liberation of Afghanistan, welcome as it was, was a side issue. The purpose for which the American-led coalition launched the war was to destroy or capture the leaders of Islamist terror, and start annihilating their forces. In terms of the war's real purpose, liberating Afghanistan from the Taliban has only been of secondary importance.

Militant Islam is not there, but here. The terrorist enemy has no armies to send against us; it has to penetrate our perimeter through fifth columnists. The troops of terrorism are disguised as students, visitors, or residents. In a war with terrorism, invading Afghanistan can be less meaningful than invading New Jersey. And while invading New Jersey in a literal sense may not be necessary or possible, it's not only possible but necessary to understand that in this war the enemy's most dangerous troop concentrations are inside our borders, not outside.

This isn't to minimize the importance of taking the action to the enemy's home bases. It's important to deal with those who finance, indoctrinate, supply, and shelter terrorists, many of whom may well reside in Iran, Iraq, Afghanistan, Pakistan, or Saudi Arabia. The training camps of al Qaeda were in Afghanistan (among other places) until recently. But while al Qaeda's training camps are abroad, its combat troops are in New Jersey, Michigan, Ontario, and Quebec.

Losing sight of this can result in losing the war against terrorism. Even at best, it can result in prolonging the war and making it more costly than necessary. In every war the enemy needs to be met and defeated in the field, and the field in this war isn't in faraway places, but in the cities, towns, and neighbourhoods of the West.

In Afghanistan the terrorists are virtually powerless against the forces arrayed against them. They might ambush some U.S. patrols or shoot down a helicopter or two, but that's about all. In Manhattan and Washington, however, terrorists and defenders are evenly matched. The terrorists' ability to strike stealthily and unexpectedly may actually give them the upper hand.

The same is true of other countries. We now know that Islamic militants in Canada tried to join al Qaeda and Taliban fighters in Afghanistan. "The numbers are small but there are some," Ward Elcock, director of the Canadian Security Intelligence Service (CSIS) was quoted as saying this week. No doubt the numbers are small, but in wars of terror a few can do a great deal. It would take millions of enemy marines and paratroopers to invade New York and Washington (assuming they could do it at all), but it only took nineteen terrorists to blow up part of the Pentagon and Lower Manhattan. One militant lurking behind the lines has the military value of a thousand regular soldiers. The few who CSIS says were ready to join al Qaeda in Afghanistan, are ready to do al Qaeda's work right here in Canada.

Liberating Afghanistan is all very well, but during the last decade the West has liberated various Muslim populations or defended them against their enemies, both Muslim and non-Muslim. During the 1990s, U.S.-led coalitions liberated Kuwait and shielded Saudi Arabia against Iraq, then continued protecting Iraq's own Kurdish and Shiite population against Saddam Hussein, then championed and defended (and continue championing and defending) the Muslims of Bosnia and Kosovo against their Serb, Croat, and Macedonian neighbours. During the same period, the U.S. tried also to save Somalia's Sunni Muslim population from starvation, dispensed billions in aid to Egypt, and attempted to bring about the creation of a Palestinian state in the Middle East.

In return for America's efforts to feed Somalia, aid Egypt, defend Bosnia and Kosovo, and broker peace at Madrid, Oslo, and Camp David, Islamist forces slaughtered a U.S. helicopter crew in Mogadishu, blew up two U.S. embassies in Africa, attacked a battleship in Yemen, bombed the World Trade Center in 1993, and finally visited September 11 on America. To say that being helpful to Muslims hasn't benefited the West is putting it mildly.

If only 0.1 per cent of all Muslims who reside in North America are willing to participate in militant acts against the West, or support in some material way the ones who do, it means that Osama bin Laden has thousands of troops at his disposal right in our midst. It's fine to think about military measures in the context of Afghanistan, Iraq, or Iran, but only as long as we remember that the enemy has already penetrated our lines. The war against terrorism cannot be won in Kabul or Baghdad without it being won in London, Detroit, and Montreal.

THE EVIL EMPIRE'S NEW ADDRESS

CanWest News Service, June 5, 2002

The thirty-nine people, including twelve children, who died last month in the Russian republic of Dagestan weren't the first victims of Islamist terror in the region. When militants exploded eleven pounds of TNT along the route of a parade commemorating Victory Day over the Nazis in World War II, they were just writing another chapter in the conflict that began with an invasion of the Botlikh region of Dagestan by militants from Chechnya on August 7, 1999.

The leader of the Islamists, Shamil Basayev, vowed at the time to expel the "infidels" form the North Caucasus. By "infidels" he meant non-Muslims. Basayev's forces declared themselves to be the government of "Independent Islamic Dagestan." Since then, Muslim secessionist attempts, coupled with Russia's efforts to eradicate them, claimed thousands of civilian lives in the region.

My reason for raising this just as Russia has become the newest (junior) member of NATO is this: the news in the West tends to be dominated by the Palestinian-Israeli conflict. The fact is, though, that if Israel didn't exist, our times would still be characterized by clashes between the Islamic and non-Islamic world.

As Professor Bernard Lewis pointed out in his Donner Canadian Foundation lecture in Toronto last week, conflicts have been alternately smouldering and raging at Islam's perimeters all over the globe. Some principal flash points have been well covered by the media; some have hardly been noted. Kashmir and Kosovo are examples of the former; Dagestan and the Chinese province of Xinjiang are examples of the latter.

Few people are unaware of the conflict between Pakistan and India over Kashmir—not surprisingly, since the clash is threatening to erupt in the first nuclear war in history (the explosions over Hiroshima and Nagasaki, devastating as they were, were atomic, not nuclear).

Muslim ambitions in the Balkans, whether for autonomy or for dominance, have been fully covered by the press—again, not surprisingly, since they've been supported by the West, not just diplomatically but militarily. NATO ended up going to war in the Balkans, first to secure Muslim Bosnia's desire for independence, then Muslim Kosovo's desire for secession, or perhaps union with Muslim Albania.

Far less has been written about Dagestan, or Xinjiang, or Indonesia's North Maluku and Central Sulawesi regions. In Indonesia, scores of Christians were murdered by "Laskar Jihad," an Indonesian Islamist movement, last year. In the village of Lata-Lata, for instance, 1,300 Christians were held hostage and given the choice of conversion to Islam or death. Though Lata-Lata's Christians were rescued after eighteen months, many others were not so lucky.

Xinjiang in northern China is at one end of an Islamic continuum that extends northwest into Kazakhstan, Uzbekistan, and eventually the North Caucasus, and southwest into Afghanistan, Pakistan, Iran, Turkey, and ultimately the Middle East. The total Muslim population of Xinjiang is about thirty-five million, of whom some five million are Uighurs (also known as Taranchis or Kashgarliks). Some Uighurs had come under the sway of militant Islam. According to China, Uighur separatists have been responsible for two hundred violent incidents in the last eleven years.

Dagestan, a poor region of the Russian Federation, is at the other end of the Islamic continuum. It neighbours Chechnya. Its population of about two million people, mainly Muslims, belong to over thirty different indigenous ethnic groups (Chechens, Laks, Avars, Dargins, etc.) speaking twenty-seven different languages. Dagestan's backwardness and tribal diversity are naturally troubled waters for Islamic militants to fish in.

This, by the way, is only to describe the Islamist impulse, not to fault it. Nations require organizing principles. Such principles are readily provided by shared ethnicity, culture, and language in some regions, but not in others. Their absence usually calls for a substitute, such as a shared dynasty, ideology, or religion. The collapse of the Soviet organizing principle in multi-ethnic regions of Russia created a vacuum for Islam to fill. Islam can't be faulted for doing so, only for blowing up civilians, including women and children, in the process.

The point is, the conflict between Palestinians and Israelis isn't the cause of the clash between the Islamic and non-Islamic world. It's merely a flash point on a long front that extends from the Black Sea to the Altai Mountains, and from Kashmir to Kosovo. Though this larger battle dares not speak its name, it will probably define the coming period, just as the previous period was defined by a clash between Nazi- or Soviet-type systems and the free world. The evil empire hasn't vanished, only changed its address.

THE DANCE OF THE CLUMSY GIANTS

National Post, June 6, 2002

Some say that if it weren't for India and Pakistan having nuclear weapons, they'd be in a shooting war by now. After all, the two countries resorted to arms three times before:

first in 1947–48, then in 1965, and the last time in 1971. The issue was always the same: Kashmir.

The difference this time? Nuclear weapons.

In 1947, Kashmir was a princely state with a Hindu ruler and a majority Muslim population. The former British Raj split into two countries after independence, a mainly Hindu India and an essentially Muslim Pakistan. The maharajas, nawabs, and bahadurs of various principalities had the choice of remaining independent or ceding their states to either country. The maharaja of Kashmir, whose Muslim subjects were about to revolt with the help of Pakistani "volunteers," chose to cede his state to India. Whether or not he was entitled to do so—in the Pakistani view, the maharaja wasn't a hereditary ruler, but just a faux-prince, appointed by the British—India responded with alacrity, pushing the Muslim volunteers back across the line. The first war ended with a truce in 1949, arranged by the United Nations.

The negotiations that followed were abandoned in 1954. This wasn't surprising, as the issue wasn't capable of resolution. Kashmir was—is—a jewel, and both India and Pakistan wanted it. Moreover, both countries felt that they had a colour of right. Kashmir's 90 per cent Muslim majority could claim that Kashmir should have gone to Pakistan in the first place, since under the original agreement all regions with a 70 per cent Muslim majority would belong to Pakistan. Princely states were an exception—which India felt Kashmir was, and Pakistan felt it wasn't, at least not legitimately.

During the second war, which began in the spring of 1965, it took until the early fall before India and Pakistan would escalate their skirmishes into air raids on each other's cities. Eventually a ceasefire was negotiated in Tashkent, a town in what was then the U.S.S.R. and is now Uzbekistan. The Tashkent Declaration resolved nothing, but kept the guns silent until 1971.

In that year, a civil war erupted in Pakistan, eventually resulting in the creation of an independent East Pakistan, called Bangladesh. The conflict also resulted in ten million East Pakistani Bengalis fleeing to India, creating a refugee nightmare. India attacked both East and West Pakistan then Pakistan bombed India's airfields in Kashmir. The clumsy giants groped at each other before Pakistan finally retreated, having suffered the loss of about one hundred thousand soldiers.

Naturally, the issue of Kashmir remained as unresolved as ever.

Is there an equitable solution? Under Wilsonian ideals of national self-determination, Kashmir would either go to Pakistan or become independent. In any referendum one of these options would carry the day. It would be a woeful day, though, for Kashmir's minorities. As it is, they've been enduring terrorism and pogroms at the hands of Islamist militants. Between 1989 and 1991 almost four hundred thousand Kashmiri Pandits were pushed out from their native valleys by terrorists, aided by Pakistan. This example of ethnic cleansing, unlike Kosovo, had gone virtually unre-marked in the West. The Kashmiri Pandits have lived as refugees in their own country, without stirring NATO to action, illustrating the likely future of minorities under mil-itant Islamic rule.

It's possible that, in the absence of nuclear weapons, India would by now have offered a military response to the suicide car bombing of the Jammu and Kashmir state par-liaments last November that claimed forty victims, not to mention the terrorist assault on India's own parliament in New Delhi that claimed the lives of nine police officers. The attackers certainly had the backing of factions in Pakistan, even allowing for the possibility that they didn't have the backing of President Pervez Musharraf himself.

A conventional engagement between the two nations, the second and sixth most populous in the world, could result in casualties numbering hundreds of thousands. Arguably, this is how many lives have been saved by the exis-tence of nuclear weapons in the region.

It's not an argument that I would make, though. The problem with nuclear weapons (other than the self-evident problem that they could kill millions during an exchange) is that as deterrents they're predicated on second-strike capability.

A limited number of undispersed nuclear weapons increases rather than decreases the chances of their being used in a conflict. As long as neither side has the capacity to strike back after a nuclear attack, the side that strikes first might expect to win. This increases the temptation, especially for the weaker side (in this case Pakistan), to get in the first blow. Realizing this may, of course, tempt the stronger side to strike first.

At present India and Pakistan have just enough nuclear power to make its use likely. To escape the danger zone, they'd either have to take a step forward or a step back.

The step forward, second-strike capability, is technologically difficult. The step back, nuclear disarmament, is psychologically impossible. Between the impossible and the difficult the choice is obvious, but technological development takes time, and both countries are running out of it. What makes India's and Pakistan's options even less enviable is that their nuclear neighbours, Russia and China, aren't likely to view their aspiration to membership in the second-strike club with any enthusiasm. Either way, the clumsy giants of the subcontinent may soon rue the day when they've lost their nuclear virginity.

MULTICULTURALISM'S VOLATILE MIX

National Post, June 21, 2002

The loyalty of immigrants has been remarkable in Western societies. Canada and the United States have both benefited from it. Lately, however, we've been witnessing a new phenomenon: the immigrant of dubious loyalty. We've also begun to see disloyal native-borns, whether of immigrant ancestry or Islamic conversion. It hasn't happened overnight. To see it in context, it's useful to look at the point of departure.

During World War I, with statistically insignificant exceptions, immigrants from enemy countries as well as their children remained loyal to Canada and the U.S. throughout the hostilities.

During World War II, although we treated German, Italian, or Japanese immigrants and their descendants shabbily, as a rule they responded with unfailing patriotism. For every Tokyo Rose (the American GI's nickname for Ikuko Toguri, a Japanese-American woman, born in Los Angeles, who broadcast Japanese propaganda during the war) there were thousands of Japanese-American soldiers who gave their lives to fight Fascism.

Some Jews and anti-Fascists who escaped Germany or occupied Europe ended up in Canada or America. Much as these refugees were on our side in the war against Hitler, technically they were enemy aliens. On arrival, they were often placed in internment camps. Many Canadians and Americans of Japanese, Italian, etc., extraction were interned as well, especially on the West Coast. Decades later Canada apologized, first to the Japanese and eventually to the Italian community. But—and this is the point—even our small-minded conduct failed to alter the fundamental loyalties of these immigrant groups.

The pattern continued during the Cold War, when former nationals of hostile Communist countries often found refuge in North America. These newcomers of various ethnicity and religion, from Eastern Europe to Vietnam, were at least as supportive of the values and interests of their adopted countries as native-born citizens of Western descent. Few Americans opposed the anti-American antics of Fidel Castro as resolutely, for instance, as Florida's ex-Cuban community.

Over the last thirty years, however, a new type of immigrant emerged. He seemed ready to share the West's wealth, but not its values. In many ways he resembled an invader more than a settler or a refugee. In addition to immigrant societies like Canada or the U.S., the new type affected homogenous countries such as Britain, France, and Holland as well.

Most newcomers continued to be loyal, needless to say. Conflicting loyalties influenced only a fraction—except this fraction was no longer statistically insignificant.

Instead of making efforts to assimilate—or accept the cultural consequences of not joining the mainstream, like such previous groups as the Mennonites—the new type of immigrant demanded changes in the host country's culture. He called on society to accommodate his linguistic or religious requirements.

Sometimes the matter was minor. In 1985, for instance, a Sikh CNR railway worker named Bhinder refused to exchange his turban for a regulation hard hat. Sometimes it wasn't such a minor matter: In 1991, a newly appointed Toronto police board commissioner of Asian extraction, Susan Eng, declined to take the traditional oath to the Queen.

Minor or not, the host societies' usual response was accommodation. Turbans were substituted for hard hats; the language of the police oath was changed. But accommodation only escalated demands. Requests for cultural exemption were soon followed by openly voiced sentiments of disloyalty. By the late 1990s, a Muslim group in Britain called al-Muhajiroun (Émigrés), led by Sheikh Omar Bakri Mohammed, saw fit to express the view that no British Muslim has any obligation to British law when it conflicts with the law of Allah.

Disturbing as such talk was, it wasn't unlawful. Dissent was within our democratic tradition, although the tradition presumed that the dissenters would be democrats themselves. Alas, the new dissenters were anything but. Some were terrorists, or their cheerleaders. Eventually their "dissent" culminated in the massacre of 9/11. Most of the Muslim militants who crashed airliners into Washington and New York were legal residents in America.

How did this come about? Three reasons seem to stand out. The first two have to do with our culture, the third with the culture of militant Islam.

When we retreated from the principle that immigration should serve the interests of the host country first, our misguided liberalism opened a Pandora's box. Embracing the idea of non-traditional immigration, we seemed to forget that when groups of distant cultural and political traditions arrive in significant numbers, they may establish their own communities not merely as colourful expressions of ethnic diversity—festivals or restaurants—but as separate cultural-political entities.

Next, we tried to turn this liability into an asset by promoting multiculturalism. We stopped ascribing any value to integration, and began flirting with the notion that host countries aren't legitimate entities with their own cultures, only political frameworks for various co-existing cultures. To paraphrase William Blake, instead of trying to build Jerusalem in "England's green and pleasant land," we switched to building Beirut.

Finally, in fundamentalist Islam, we've come up against a culture for which the very concept of rendering to Caesar what is Caesar's and to God what is God's is alien. Puritanical Islam considers that everything belongs to God (or rather, some mullah's idea of God). This concept doesn't allow for a secular or territorial entity, such as a country, to command a higher loyalty than one's faith. If one's religious leader demands the suppression of what he regards as a blasphemous book, the fact that Western constitutions protect free expression is just so much piffle for a true believer. His ultimate goal is a faith-based state, an Islamic theocracy.

Commenting on non-traditional immigration requires a footnote. The problem doesn't arise when people come to Canada from the Levant; the problem arises when people come to recreate the Levant in Canada. That's where non-traditional immigration and multiculturalism become a volatile mix. Extending our values to others is one thing, but modifying our values to suit the values of others is a vastly different proposition. As the late scholar Ernest van den Haag pointed out in 1965, patriotism is not racism. "The wish to preserve one's identity and the identity of one's nation," he wrote in a prescient piece in the *National Review*, "requires no justification any more than the wish to have one's own children."

By now multiculturalism has made it difficult to safeguard our traditions and ideals against a new type of immigrant whose goal is not to fit in, but to carve out a niche for his own tribe, language, customs, or religion in our country—or rather in what we're no longer supposed to view as a country but something between Grand Central Station and an empty space. When Canada is no longer regarded as a culture, with its own traditions and narratives, but a tabula rasa, a clean slate, for anyone to write on what he will, immigrants of the new school will be ready with their own texts, including some that aren't very pleasant. The sound you hear is the sharpening of their chisels.

THE VIEW FROM THE FENCE

CanWest News Service, August 28, 2002

Looking uneasily at the impending confrontation between the United States and Saddam Hussein, the European Union is trying to sit on the fence. It's not surprising. The big bang of 9/11 occurred in Washington and New York, but Europe has been experiencing the threat of Middle Eastern militancy for years. Bombings, assassinations, hijackings, and similar acts of terror, though not on the scale of the destruction of the World Trade Center, have been commonplace in Europe since the 1970s.

It was exactly twenty years ago, in August 1982, that terrorists killed six and injured twenty-two in an attack on a restaurant in Paris. A year earlier (August 1981) they killed two and injured seventeen in a Viennese synagogue. In October 1982, they killed a child and injured ten in Rome. These attacks were the work of the recently deceased Abu Nidal—the Osama bin Laden of his day—but he was by no means alone. Between August 1980 and November 1981 at least twenty acts of terrorism had been recorded in Rome, Paris, Beirut, Nairobi, Cairo, Buenos Aires, Istanbul, Vienna, Athens, and Antwerp. They killed thirty-six people and wounded hundreds. In addition to Abu Nidal's Black June, these acts were committed by such groups as Saiqua, George Habash's Popular Front, and the then-current 15 of May Movement for the Liberation of Palestine.

Militants exported their region's conflict to every corner of the world. When Pan Am Flight 103 was blown out of the sky, it killed villagers as far away from the West Bank as Lockerbie, Scotland. In the case of the writer Salman Rushdie, the deadly threat of a fatwa was directed against a citizen of the U.K.

Though acts of terror can create a steely resolve in some cultures to resist the terrorists, terror can also, as its name implies, terrorize people. It has clearly done so in Europe.

Bombs aren't the militants' only weapons of intimidation. Some Arab/Muslim pressure groups utilize the host culture's own institutions to shape the political climate. In France, the novelist Michel Houellebecq is currently being sued for making "insulting" remarks about Islam in his latest book. The plaintiffs include Saudi Arabia's World Islamic League and the Mosque of Paris.

According to BBC news, this isn't merely a civil suit. Houellebecq's remarks are claimed to contravene French legislation compelling "religious tolerance" and outlawing "racial hatred." The head of the Paris mosque, Dalil Boubakeur, is quoted as saying that Muslims feel insulted by a character in Houellebecq's novel who feels "a quiver of glee" every time a Palestinian terrorist is killed. If a court agrees that feeling gleeful about the demise of a Palestinian terrorist, or merely describing such a person in a novel, is against French law, Houellebecq—who recently won the prestigious IMPAC award—could face a year in jail.

Meanwhile in Denmark, as reported by Daniel Pipes and Lars Hedegaard, "Muslim leaders openly declare their goal of introducing Islamic law once Denmark's Muslim population grows large enough." In anticipation of that happy day, the militant Islamist organization Hizb-ut-Tahrir is contending itself with calling on Muslims "to kill Jews... wherever you find them."

The Danish state prosecutor is thinking about banning Hizb-ut-Tahrir. The risk, I suppose, is that doing so might flout some European human rights–type legislation compelling "religious tolerance."

Twelve years ago, as the Soviet Union's imminent collapse was greeted with euphoria, I sounded a cautionary note. I wrote that even if all the Marxist-type tyrannies and the West's own loony left were to run out of steam together, mankind's totalitarian impulse still wouldn't come to an end.

"It's possible to do away with an evil empire," I wrote in 1990, "but it's much harder to do away with evil. Greed, fear, stupidity, selfishness, paranoia, intolerance, sloth, envy, and all our other deadly sins are here to stay. No doubt they'll find new flags in which to wrap themselves.

"The most likely new candidates for evil? After our experience of black, brown, and red fascism, I wouldn't exclude the greens. In fact, two varieties of greens: The fanatics of the environment, and the fanatics of Islam."

Some of Islam's fanatics have settled in Europe, but it hasn't turned them into Europeans. They've become adept at making use of the West's values without sharing them. The World Islamic League sues for religious tolerance for Muslims, while Hizb-ut-Tahrir issues calls to kill Jews. And Europeans who invited unbridled immigration are painfully learning to sit on the fence they neglected to use for its original purpose.

ISLAM'S MALFORMED KIN
National Post, October 8, 2002

Now that the hunt for Osama bin Laden has begun, it may be of interest to note that he and his network al Qaeda aren't without antecedents in the history of Islam. In 1090, just a few years before the first Crusade, a native of Qom named Hasan ibn Al-Sabah acquired a fortress high in the Elburz mountains in present-day Iran. In Alamut ("eagle's nest"), Al-Sabah and his acolytes established an offshoot of the Ismaili sect of Shiite Islam.

This sub-sect sent out young Muslim fanatics to kill their opponents as a religious duty. Its devotees became known by a name that went into English as a synonym for a politically motivated murderer: Assassin.

Some scholars say the word comes from the Arabic *hassasin*, or "hashish user," because the young terrorists, by taking the drug, simulated the pleasures of paradise that was to be their reward for killing and dying for their cause.

Others suggest the name comes from the Arabic *assassiyun* or "fundamentalist," from the word *assass*, or "foundation."

Or "base," as in "al Qaeda." As an educated man, Mr. bin Laden would be thoroughly familiar with the history of the Assassins.

Al-Sabah was an ascetic who combined austerity with assassination. He was as strict with himself as with his enemies: He had both of his sons killed, one for unauthorized murder, and the other for drinking wine. The daggers of his suicide squads spread terror from Persia to Syria. One Muslim scholar, when asked why he stopped denouncing the sect, replied that it was because the Assassins' arguments were "both pointed and weighty."

The Venetian traveller Marco Polo, who visited the region around 1272, long after Al-Sabah's death, but while the Assassins were still plying their trade, described the sect and its young "suicide-bombers" this way: "[W]hen the Old Man would have any prince slain, he would say to such a youth: 'Go thou and slay So and So; and when thou returnest my Angels shall bear thee into Paradise.'"*

Last Saturday, Harvard law professor Alan Dershowitz tried to reduce a clash of civilizations to an American prosecutor's opening to a jury. "We will prove to you," Mr. Dershowitz thundered in his moot court, "that bin Laden has intention—as clearly as Hitler did in *Mein*

* Some scholar's dispute Marco Polo's account.

Kampf—to kill as many Americans, Jews, and their allies as he is able to."

Not a very difficult task, I'd say, considering Mr. bin Laden's own declarations. "We are sure of our victory against the Americans and the Jews as promised by the Prophet," Mr. bin Laden explained to John Miller of *Esquire* magazine in February 1999. "Judgment day shall not come until the Muslim fights the Jew, where the Jew will hide behind trees and stones, and the tree and the stone will speak and say, 'Muslim, behind me is a Jew. Come and kill him.'"

Mr. bin Laden has been rather open about everything Mr. Dershowitz proposes to prove against him. He intends to kill Americans, Jews, and what he calls "crusaders" whether they're combatants or non-combatants ("we do not differentiate between those dressed in military uniforms and civilians; they are all targets in this fatwa") not because he likes doing it, but because he believes that killing the infidel is his destiny.

As he told ABC News producer Rahimullah Yousafzai in December 1998, "[K]illing and fighting have been prescribed for us, by the Grace of God, who says in his holy book 'fighting is prescribed for you, and ye dislike it. But it is possible that ye dislike a thing, which is good for you, and that ye love a thing which is bad for you. But God knoweth and you know not.'"

This is what Mr. bin Laden believes. It's also his message to other believers. "As I have stated before, it is our job to instigate," he said to Mr. Yousafzai. And he added to Mr. Miller a year later: "It is our duty to lead people to the light."

Is this conspiracy to incite violence? Such petty legal terms are no more appropriate to Mr. bin Laden's utterances than they would have been to Pope Urban II's sermon at Clermont in 1095, launching the first Crusade. Drawing a parallel between Pope Urban II and Mr. bin Laden isn't falling into the trap of moral equivalence. The parallel exists because they both have eleventh-century minds—the pope legitimately, of course, because he lived in the eleventh century.

Mr. bin Laden may live in the computer age, but he harbours eleventh-century sentiments. And the thing about eleventh-century sentiments is that—while it may become necessary to kill someone for harbouring them—they're not a crime.

Of course, questioning Mr. bin Laden's criminality doesn't mean that Americans, Jews, or the West in general should meekly submit to him and his holy assassins. On the contrary: Mr. bin Laden and his followers should be annihilated. It's only absurd to try them in Mr. Dershowitz's moot court.

In a real trial, Mr. bin Laden might be acquitted for a variety of legal and procedural reasons, no matter how instrumental he was in the murder of thousands of Americans and others. The only trial in which acquittal is unthinkable is a show trial. Why would we risk either a) acquitting a mortal enemy, or b) demeaning our legal system by holding a show trial? Mortal enemies aren't to be tried, but destroyed.

The next question concerns Mr. bin Laden's relationship to Islam.

"We will continue this course because it is a part of our religion, and because God, Praise and Glory be to him, ordered us to carry out jihad so that the word of God may remain exalted to the heights," he told Mr. Yousafzai in 1998, adding, "If the instigation for jihad against the Jews and the Americans is considered a crime, let history be a witness that I am a criminal."

Moderate Arab politicians and Islamic scholars, together with politicians and pundits in the West, dismiss such utterances as un-Islamic heresy. It would certainly be comforting, as well as tactically expedient, to regard Mr. bin Laden as an apostate, but it may not be accurate. It may even be intellectually dishonest.

"Heresy" is what all sides accuse each other of in any dispute, religious or secular. All sides can quote the holy books in support of their positions. In any event, Islam isn't as centralized a doctrine as some other major religions. Muslims don't necessarily submit to one ecclesiastical authority. The mere fact that many believers don't agree with Mr. bin Laden's neo-medievalism doesn't make him a heretic.

Some scholars say the closest to the Christian concept of heresy in Islam is *bid'a*, or "innovation." There's a saying attributed to the Prophet, quoted by Bernard Lewis in his 1976 book *Islam and the Arab World*: "The worst things are those that are novelties. Every novelty is an innovation, every innovation is an error and every error leads to hell-fire."

As one who detests trendiness, I'm not without sympathy to the Prophet's observation. Still, it's easy to see how such a notion would logically lead to both a visceral aversion to modernity and a resurgence of neo-medievalism within Islam.

The suggestion that Islamists—that is, Muslims who resist modern ideals to the point of calling for a jihad or holy struggle against them—merely twist the teachings of the Koran and are somehow alien to Islam, isn't borne out by the evidence. The followers of bin Laden, the Taliban, and other Muslim fundamentalists appear to be a historically legitimate branch of the tree of Islam. The Western world's enemy isn't Islam as such, but militant fundamentalism—except while militant fundamentalism may be dormant in all religions, in our day it's awake only in one.

At the same time "Islamism = Islam" isn't the equation either. Now that the shooting war has begun, some Islamic countries will be in the forefront of fighting Islamist forces, just as Western countries were in the forefront of fighting and ultimately defeating both Nazism and Communism. Yet, as John O'Sullivan pointed out, Nazism and Communism were malformed offshoots of Western civilization, not something apart from it. Similarly, Islamism is Islam's malformed kin. We can only hope that Islam will help to resist and defeat it, just as the West had defeated its own monstrous progenies.

TERRORISM'S LATEST CRITIC

National Post, October 29, 2002

It was amusing, in a grim sort of way, to see Saddam Hussein emerge last week as one of the severest critics of the Chechen terror action in Moscow. "This will give Zionism and America the chance to undermine Islam and Muslims," he warned the late Movsar Barayev and his co-ed terrorists getting ready to blow up hostages in a theatre.

The last thing the tyrant of Iraq needed was for fanatics to create difficulties for Russia's Vladimir Putin, just at the time when Mr. Putin was the only thing standing between Saddam and annihilation—or one of very few things, anyway. With George W. Bush on the warpath, Saddam's corner was being rapidly emptied. Not counting the appeasers at the *New York Times* or in Kofi Annan's suite in the United Nations, there were only China, France, and Russia with their UN Security Council vetoes as potential roadblocks to regime change in Iraq.

No wonder Saddam seemed wistful last week. His hopes for Russia's veto, never a certainty, probably vanished with the terrorists' attempt to blackmail Mr. Putin by threatening to murder seven hundred Muscovites. Saddam knew that the latest Islamist outrage would increase the chances of Mr. Putin making a deal with Mr. Bush, giving, in effect, Russia a freer hand in Chechnya in exchange for staying its veto in the UN.

"It is not wise that the Chechens lose the sympathy of the Russians," sighed the sage of Baghdad in an appeal he said was addressed to "Muslims in general and Chechens in particular." His advice came too late. The Chechens had lost the sympathy of the Russians long before a flawed rescue attempt turned the Moscow hostage-taking into a tragedy.

In today's climate, small entities with their assorted gripes and ambitions—legitimate or otherwise—are losing the sympathy of their neighbours. In our age of terrorism, people feel less threatened by big-power rivalries than by the ambitions, insecurities, jealousies, and grievances of minor nations and tribes jockeying for position around the edges of contemporary history. Their aspirations or laments constitute a menace to the stability of regions in which the major powers have finally achieved a precarious balance.

This was illustrated in recent weeks by the admission of North Korea's "Dear Leader," Kim Jong-Il, that he cheated on his 1994 deal with the naive appeasers of the West. Contrary to an agreement cobbled together by former president Jimmy Carter, the latest winner of the tarnished Nobel Peace Prize, Kim blithely went on with North Korea's nuclear weapons development program. According to some intelligence estimates, the Far Eastern link in Mr. Bush's axis of evil already possesses two fifteen-kiloton bombs—not huge as nuclear devices go, but enough to blow a much bigger hole in the middle of Manhattan than al Qaeda did on September 11.

Dear Leader's confession seemed like a godsend to assorted promoters of dithering. They latched on to North Korea's nukes to argue that since Kim Jong-Il, whom Mr. Bush wasn't proposing to forcibly disarm, was a more acute threat, it made no sense to disarm Saddam. The ditherers were careful not to carry their argument to its logical conclusion, which would have been to urge Mr. Bush to disarm Kim Jong-Il instead. There was no danger, though, of logic playing any part in appeasement politics. What the proliferation of nuclear weapons among unstable tyrants indicated to Neville Chamberlain's heirs was that the West should disarm tyrants even less and dither even more.

Luckily, given the current occupant of the White House, Chamberlain's heirs remain only of academic interest for the time being. Less fortunately, North Korea's nuclear program threatens grave consequences for the future of Taiwan.

The reason is simple. North Korea is in a tough neighbourhood. Mr. Putin and Chinese president Jiang Zemin aren't keen on having a nuclear Kim in their backyard; certainly no keener than Japanese prime minister Junichiro Koizumi or South Korean president Kim Dae-jung. Neither Mr. Zemin, nor his likely successor, Vice-President Hu Jintao, need a competitor. If there's any nuclear blackmailing to be done in their neck of the woods, they prefer to do it themselves.

It's a safe bet that during the Texas meeting last weekend between Mr. Bush and the seventy-six-year-old Mr. Zemin the topic of North Korea came up. (Mr. Putin would have attended, too, but thanks to the late Mr. Barayev and his explosive ladies, he was otherwise engaged.) It's a similarly safe bet that Mr. Zemin agreed to help Mr. Bush persuade Dear Leader to give up his nuclear program—for a price.

Mr. Zemin's price is likely to include a freer hand in annexing Taiwan, just as Mr. Putin's price would include a freer hand in hanging on to Chechnya. These are offers Mr. Bush may not cherish, but can't refuse.

There's a black cloud of *realpolitik* casting a shadow over Taiwan. Few people have noticed it yet, but Barbara Amiel has. She remarked in her *Daily Telegraph* column on Monday: "If I were a Taiwanese resident, it might be time to check out my visas."

THE MUSLIM NATION

National Post, November 15, 2002

When the audio tape attributed to Osama bin Laden was released last week, the voice that threatened America's allies didn't issue its warning in the name of al Qaeda. It didn't purport to speak for Iraq, Indonesia, Chechnya, Afghanistan, or the Palestinian territories. Though the voice listed them all, it spoke for what it called "the Muslim nation."

"As you assassinate," Mr. bin Laden said to the West, naming each of six countries in turn, from Australia to Great Britain, and from Canada to Italy, "so will you be assassinated. As you bomb so will you likewise be. So the Muslim nation begins to attack you with its children, who are committed before God to continue the jihad, by word and by the sword..."

About two days later U.S. president George W. Bush also made a set of remarks as he began a meeting with UN secretary-general Kofi Annan.

"By far, the vast majority of American citizens respect the Islamic people and the Muslim faith," Mr. Bush said, while dissociating his government from intemperate comments about Muslims made by some televangelists, whom Mr. Bush didn't name. The president probably referred to Pat Robertson who reportedly said recently that Muslims were "worse than the Nazis" or to Jerry Falwell who in a TV interview last month described the prophet Muhammad as a "terrorist."

"It is encouraging to hear President Bush address the issue of Islamophobic rhetoric in our society. We hope the president's rejection of anti-Muslim hate speech will be followed by similar statements from other elected officials and from mainstream religious leaders," commented CAIR communications director Ibrahim Hooper.

No disagreement here. It's indeed encouraging for the general cause of peace and tolerance in the world that President Bush repudiates excessive or thoughtless statements and reaffirms fundamental Western values. But it would be equally reassuring for leaders of Islamic countries, from Egypt to Saudi Arabia, to have issued similar statements following the speech attributed to Osama bin Laden.

It would have been reassuring to hear one or more major figures in the world of Islam to say that "the vast majority of citizens of Muslim countries respect the American people and the Christian faith." Except this didn't happen. Nor did CAIR communications director Ibrahim Hooper express the hope that it might happen. He didn't offer to repudiate what Osama bin Laden said while purporting to speak for the "Muslim nation." Mr. Hooper expected "other elected officials and mainstream religious leaders" to follow the president's example and declare that Pat Robertson and other televangelists don't speak for America, but he didn't offer to declare, or call on Muslim leaders to declare, that "Mr. bin Laden doesn't speak for Islam."

So what we're left with is Mr. bin Laden declaring that he speaks for the "Muslim nation," which now "begins to attack you with its children," without anybody saying, "No, Mr. bin Laden, you do not. You do not speak for the millions of peace-loving Muslims. You speak only for a handful of terrorists."

So far we've heard nothing from the millions of peace-loving Muslims. We've heard nothing from their political leaders in Islamic countries. We've heard nothing from their spiritual leaders, whether at home or in the West. We've heard nothing from the spokespeople of CAIR. If it weren't for President Bush's assurance that millions of peace-loving Muslims exist, we wouldn't know it. They're silent, except when some exhort us, like Mr. Hooper, to keep declaring through our "elected officials and mainstream religious leaders" that Muslims are peace-loving.

I don't doubt that they are, only I wouldn't mind hearing it from them for a change. It was great to hear it from President Bush, but now I'd like to hear it from CAIR.

Whatever Pat Robertson said, he blew up nothing. However injudicious Jerry Falwell's remarks have been, he didn't threaten anyone with assassination. Robertson or Falwell cannot be mentioned in the same breath with Osama bin Laden—yet as soon as they spoke, the president dissociated his government and his country from them. "I'll remind the secretary-general," he said, "that our war against terror is a war against individuals whose hearts are full of hate. We do not fight a religion."

Did Muslim leaders, secular or religious, say anything to dissociate themselves and their faith from Mr. bin Laden when he declared his jihad against "the Crusaders and the Jews"? Did the ruler of a supposedly friendly Arab country, like Saudi Arabia or Jordan, say, as Mr. Bush did, that "the comments that have been uttered... do not reflect the sentiments of my government"?

When asked this question, Arab and Muslim commentators usually reply that 1) we *have* said it, and 2) why should we be obliged to say the obvious? The two replies are offered in the same breath, though reply number 1 is negated by reply number 2, and reply number 2 is worthless. On this test, President Bush shouldn't be obliged to say the obvious either (i.e., that "ours is a country based upon tolerance" and that we won't let "terrorists cause us to change our values"), yet he's not only saying it, but CAIR demands that he and other leaders should say it even louder and more often. They're right to demand it because in such situations the obvious isn't obvious unless it's stated loudly and often—except this is no less true for CAIR than for President Bush. The difference is that Mr. Bush is actually saying it, while Muslim countries and communities say little beyond reiterating their own grievances.

Sorry. Reiterating grievances isn't enough to convince the world that Mr. bin Laden is only engaged in wishful thinking when he says he speaks for "the Muslim nation."

THE FRIENDLY OILARCHY

CanWest News Service, November 27, 2002

It would be interesting to know whether the charitable Princess Haifa al Faisal, wife of Saudi ambassador Prince Bandar bin Sultan, did in fact transfer money into the bank accounts of two men who gave financial support to some 9/11 hijackers. If she did, it would be interesting to know whether she had any inkling where her money was going.

Ostensibly, the princess had been sending two thousand dollars a month to a Saudi woman living in America to help pay for her medical treatment. The FBI is now investigating whether this money ended up in the pockets of two terrorists who crashed their hijacked airliner into the Pentagon.

Interesting as the answer may be, ultimately it doesn't matter much. Whether we'll find out what the Saudi ambassador's wife did or didn't do, intentionally or unwittingly, what we've long known is more important. We've long known that the Saudis materially support radical Islam.

We've known it well before the events of 9/11. We've known what U.S. Democratic senator Charles Schumer now describes as "a duplicitous game" in which the Saudis "say to the terrorists, 'We'll do everything you want, just leave us alone.'" We've known what the outgoing chairman of the U.S. Senate Foreign Relations Committee, Senator Joseph Biden, has called a Saudi history of "buying off extremism."

On a recent CNN program, Senator Biden described it as "part of a saga where the Saudis don't know, have not checked, are not nearly conscientious enough in determining whether or not a 'charity' is genuinely a charity or a front for, or a back door for, terrorists or terrorist-sympathizing organizations or individuals."

Indeed. But the puzzle isn't why the Saudis have averted their gaze from terrorism. The puzzle is why we've been averting our gaze from what the Saudis have been doing.

The Saudis have one foot in the twenty-first century and another in the Middle Ages. Their theocratic monarchy of five thousand princes floats in a sea of oil. Though the ruling house has long embraced and fostered the Wahhabi sect, a fundamentalist version of Islam, some Saudis may be even more extreme. This makes the dynasty understandably insecure. Remembering the example of the shah of Iran, swept away by the radical Islamic revolution of the Ayatollah Khomeini, the Saudi royal family has attempted to outflank the fundamentalists on the left by being what in our culture would be called "more Catholic than the pope." Fanatics or sybarites, the Saudi royals tried to maintain a separate peace with the militants in their midst.

This often took the form of material support, either to out-and-out terrorists, or to institutions of religious extremism that have been the distilleries of fanaticism and terror. Without the direct or indirect sponsorship of the Saudi oligarchy—or should we call it "oilarchy"?—entities such as al Qaeda couldn't have flourished.

But if the Saudis closed their eyes to the terrorists, we've closed our eyes to the Saudis. We looked the other way as much as they did. We let Saudi officials distribute in America, through organizations such as the World Assembly of Muslim Youth, material that we'd call hate literature if distributed by anyone else. (Samples: "Judaism and Christianity are deviant religions" and "The unbelievers, idolaters, and others like them must be hated and despised...") According to Republican congressman Dan Burton, we looked the other way when Saudi fathers abducted American children from mixed marriages. Reportedly, we even removed a female air traffic controller from duty to spare Saudi sensibilities when Crown Prince Abdullah flew his royal jet into Waco, Texas, to visit U.S. president George W. Bush at his Crawford ranch.

Why? The usual answer is oil—as in "the West needs oil." This is true, but the West doesn't need to buy oil half as much as Middle East needs to sell it. Oil in the ground buys no Rolls-Royces. One can't feed oil to the camels. The Saudi princes' underground bounty would be of little use to them without developed countries that can afford to pay for it. We don't need to be nice to the Saudis if they're being nasty to us for the sake of oil.

Yet until now Americans have tiptoed around the Saudis in an almost Canadian way. It's this attitude to which the antics of Princess Haifa al Faisal may have put an end. Instead of worrying about alienating a duplicitous bunch of medieval zealots and playboys, the White House seems ready to make them worry—seriously worry—about alienating America.

NEEDING DANGER TO SEE THE OBVIOUS

National Post, December 1, 2002

Ferenc Molnár was the author of such international hits as *Liliom*, better known to North American audiences as the Broadway musical *Carousel* (with music and lyrics by Rodgers and Hammerstein). As the dark clouds of Nazism approached Molnár's native Budapest, he fled to America where he settled in the Plaza Hotel in New York.

Manhattan can be pretty stifling in the summer. One day a fellow refugee complained to the playwright about the humidity.

"My dear chap," Molnár replied, "we didn't come here for the climate."

Molnár's bon mot became a classic among refugees. It begs the question, though, of what most immigrants to the U.S. or Canada came in search of. If we didn't come here for the climate, what did we come for? Was it for streets paved with gold?

I'm only sure of my own answer. November 23, the day the *National Post* began its "Strong and Free" series of essays about Canada, happened to be the forty-sixth anniversary of the day I left communist Hungary. I did come for a climate of sorts: the climate of freedom. More precisely, I came to escape the oppressive climate of statist Europe.

I came to the right place, but what I didn't realize was that the climate of statism would follow me here. Like most countries, Canada has undergone tremendous changes in the last half century. Some have been for the better; some for the worse. In our efforts to get rid of the vices of stodgy old "WASP" Canada, we've managed to throw out many of its virtues. The country in which I landed in 1956 was both significantly stronger and freer than the one in which I make my home today.

Forty-six years ago, if Canadians didn't approve of something, they tended to use one of two expressions. They'd either say: "Well, it's a free country," or they'd say: "There ought to be a law."

Today, one rarely hears the first saying anymore. Most people sense that it's no longer accurate. As for the second expression, it has become superfluous. By now there *is* a law at every turn, whether there ought to be one or not.

The problem isn't the law as such. When I came to Canada, the courts were using the law as a bulwark to protect the individual against the state. It's worth noting that they did so without a Charter of Rights and Freedoms. But climate is everything: today's courts use the law as a battering ram to break down individual rights and freedoms. They justify their breach of the Charter by references to social policy.

Canada's judges used to be freedom's friends; by now they've become freedom's enemies. A few may dissent, but in almost any conflict between someone's individual rights and the ambitions of a feminist, environmentalist, multicultural, or public hygiene policy, statism will carry the day. It doesn't matter whether the state's ambitions clash with a person's right of expression, property, or conscience, it's the individual rights that lose. When the existing law isn't restrictive enough, majorities on the bench may strike it down and substitute one that Parliament, much as it might have wanted to, wouldn't have dared to pass itself.

Dirigisme, as issued from bureaucracy's Temple of Central Planning, has become the state religion of Canada. It's not surprising that when it came to looking into the fiasco of universal medical care, Prime Minister Jean Chrétien gave the task to a venerable mullah of statism, Roy Romanow. The former Ayatollah of Saskatchewan concluded that the magic formula for making a silk purse out of a sow's ear was to multiply the cost of his own study—fifteen million dollars—by a thousand, so he recommended throwing fifteen billion good dollars after the untold billions of bad dollars we spent on a fundamentally flawed idea. We're to spend this sum, along with the lives of untreated patients on medicare's waiting lists, as a human sacrifice on the altar of socialism, the faith of Mr. Romanow's formative years.

Proponents of *dirigisme* like to say that since individual freedoms tend to collide, the state must pick and choose between them. Indeed, there's no "absolute" freedom. Apologists for big government greet such self-evident truisms with shouts of "eureka" as if they were ground-breaking discoveries. It isn't hard to figure out why. Statists use the fact that there's no absolute freedom to deny us relative freedoms. Promoters of intrusive government fabricate sophistries on an assembly line to support their position. "We all exist as part of a community," is one favourite cliché. Such commonplaces are fired off at Mach 2 by those who would obscure the difference between jails and shelters, lifelines and restraints. They give us a government so caring it would sooner let people die waiting for free medical care than let them buy it for themselves. They argue that since we can't fly like birds, the state has an excuse not to let us walk upright like human beings. The phrase "there's no absolute freedom" has become the argument of those who prefer to see us crawl.

Forty-six years after my arrival I have much to celebrate. Foremost, I celebrate that Canada is still a free country relative to many others. I also have things to mourn. Foremost, I mourn that Canada is less free than it was forty-six years ago. While it's free compared to other lands, it's not free compared to itself. The last forty-six years for me were like watching a loved one decline from robust, athletic health to moderate self-sufficiency. It's hard to cheer when, after the ravages of a progressive disease, the former champion can still brush his own teeth and tie his own shoelaces.

Ironically, the world I abandoned in my quest for freedom developed in the opposite direction. To pursue the analogy, if Canada's is the sad story of a declining athlete, post-communist Eastern Europe is a triumphant tale of a wheelchair-bound cripple taking his first halting steps. True, in terms of freedom, Hungary may not be able to brush its own teeth and tie its own shoelaces as dexterously as Canada, but it amounts to a victory that it can do it at all. The same accomplishment makes Canada a tragic caricature of its former self.

Not to end on an unhappy note, I put my faith in al Qaeda. The poet John Donne prayed that God may preserve us from needing danger to be good, but sometimes we need danger, not only to be good, but to see the obvious. We often don't know what we have until we come near losing it. The nanny state has been a grave threat to liberty, but big government's insidious emanations, whether from Ottawa, Washington, or Brussels, have passed unnoticed by many. Creeping statism may not trip the alarm. We needed a genuine jolt, and 9/11 has delivered it.

After the defeat of Nazism and Communism, nothing threatens human freedom more than the rise of a totalitarian offshoot of Islam. The enemy isn't the Muslim faithful, just as in earlier times it wasn't the ordinary people of Germany or Russia, but the fanatic ideologues who claimed to act in their name. It's ironic that it may turn out to be Osama bin Laden who unwittingly reinvigorates Western values, including the value of being strong and free, in our own hearts and minds.

2003

KOFI WORSE THREAT THAN SADDAM

National Post, January 28, 2003

In the fall of 2002, the Bush administration decided to move against Saddam Hussein through the United Nations. On September 12, the president addressed the General Assembly. "If we fail to act in the face of danger," Mr. Bush said, "the people of Iraq will continue to live in brutal submission. The regime will have new power to bully and dominate and conquer its neighbors, condemning the Middle East to more years of bloodshed and fear."

The choice to move against Saddam through the UN rather than "unilaterally" via a U.S.-led coalition of Great Britain, Australia, and others was partly motivated by a wish to save the venerable institution. Though by then the UN had long departed from its own founding principles—many of its member states were in direct opposition to free speech or periodic elections—some still hoped that the organization may be recaptured for its original purposes, such as defending the rule of law against dictatorships.

It's been alleged that the choice of "going the UN route" was urged on the Bush cabinet by Secretary of State Colin Powell against the objections of Defence Secretary Donald Rumsfeld. Be that as it may, it turned out to be the wrong choice. UN weapons inspector Hans Blix's report this week—concluding that Iraq still hasn't shown "genuine acceptance" of the demand to disarm—was too little too late. While in September the president had overwhelming support for his call that the United Nations "fulfill its promise in our time" by authorizing military action if Saddam fails to disarm, within months the UN support dissipated, carrying with it much of the support for Mr. Bush's policy even at home. Far from enhancing the mission of challenging tyrants who threaten the world's peace, the UN subverted it. The momentum was lost; the task of dealing with Saddam became harder. In September, Mr. Bush could have confronted Saddam with a support of 81 per cent of Americans if Iraq failed to cooperate with UN inspectors. Today he may have to do it with the support of about 52 per cent.

None of this has been particularly surprising. As I wrote on September 26, 2002, "Last week [U.S. president George W. Bush] delivered a tough speech, which may jolt the United Nations into action. This could have the result of rescuing the UN from irrelevance and oblivion.

"Rescuing an institution that has elected the representative of Libya as the chairman of its human rights commission is a dubious objective. Before Mr. Bush's speech, the UN was well on its way to share an urn in the mausoleum of history with the League of Nations. Doing away with Saddam is dandy, but doing away with Saddam at the price of saving the UN may not be such a smart deal."

By now it's evident that it was a lousy deal. The UN has graduated from occasionally exempting itself from its own founding principles to betraying them altogether. By now even doing away with Saddam won't serve the prospect of peace and democracy in the world as much as doing away with UN secretary-general Kofi Annan's fiefdom. If the old League of Nations foundered because it showed itself to be irrelevant when faced with the aggression of dictators like Mussolini, the UN will founder because it has become a shield for every Mussolini of our day.

In fact, by now the UN is a link in the axis of evil. Its infamous 1975 "Zionism is racism" resolution may have been rescinded, but within six years the same institution conjured up the spirit of Durban with its thinly veiled threat to push the Jews into the sea. Today it's Le Corbusier's United Nations headquarters in Manhattan that shelters the architects of the next holocaust.

America is accused of "unilateralism" these days, not only by Hollywood's lefty confuseniks, but Canada's foreign minister, Bill Graham. Looking to the moral authority of the UN, an institution that chooses Colonel Gaddafi's realm to head its human rights commission, to balance the unilateralism of the world's greatest democracy may seem like madness at first, but there's a method to it. Objections to "unilateralism" are more than just coded expressions of anti-Americanism. They're also coded expressions of opposition to Western values. They signal Europe's continued flirtation with statism, appeasement, and anti-Semitism. They denote opposition to electoral democracy, free enterprise, individual liberty, trial by jury, and even such post-Westphalian notions as national sovereignty.

It's the system of free liberal democracies that "multilateralists" hope to replace with a system of supra-national mandarins running the world through UN committees and international tribunals. They're prepared to rule in their own name and as proxies for a constituency of like-minded authoritarian regimes from Brussels to Beijing. Multilateralists envisage benevolent bureaucracies inspired by statism replacing sovereign nations of elected governments inspired by the rule of law.

As a bastion of multilateralism, the UN has become a menace—a menace, above all, to its own original principles. By now the institution's main role is to enable dysfunctional dictatorships to punch above their weight. Still, people who have high regard for the ideals that brought the UN into being continue to be on the lookout for saving graces. Some argue that the UN is a worthwhile institution, only it has been "hijacked" by coalitions of dictators, hate-mongers, and their appeasers.

True as this may be, it's meaningless. It's like saying that Islam is a peaceful religion, only it has been "hijacked" by Wahhabi sheiks, theocratic ayatollahs, and followers of Osama bin Laden. The point about a hijacked entity, whether it's a commercial jet, a great religion, or an international institution like the UN, is that once it has been diverted, it's under the hijackers' command. At this stage, regardless of its benevolent origins, regardless of its innocent passengers and crew, it becomes an instrument of destruction. A hijacked airliner is a missile on its way to the Twin Towers. If it can't be rescued from its hijackers, it must be shot down.

The same goes for a hijacked institution. Irrespective of what action Mr. Bush contemplates against Saddam, America should cut itself loose from the United Nations. It should withdraw from the world body then offer Kofi Annan and his cohorts a generous period—say, six months—to get out of town.

OLD EUROPE STRIKES BACK

National Post, March 4, 2003

We've seen the Empire strike back in the last couple of weeks—that is, the empire of what U.S. defense secretary

Donald Rumsfeld has called "old Europe." Stung by accusations that Franco-German obstruction of the Bush administration's efforts to bring about a regime change in Iraq is motivated by invidious feelings of rivalry with the sole superpower in the post–Cold War world—"phallUS-envy" for short—European commentators have made spirited efforts to defend German chancellor Gerhard Schroeder's and French president Jacques Chirac's position.

The latest salvo is a witty piece by Justin Vaisse, a visiting fellow at the Center on the U.S. and Europe at the Brookings Institution. In an article that originally appeared in the *Washington Post*, M. Vaisse sarcastically apologizes for being ungrateful to America that liberated France in World War II. "It's just that I learned in school," he writes, "that France and Britain declared war on Nazi Germany in September 1939, while the United States was enacting isolationist laws, and that America entered the war two years later, only after Japan attacked Pearl Harbor. But now I see that was just Gallic propaganda. How could I have believed it?"

M. Vaisse is evidently wounded by the suggestion that his country's attempt to thwart U.S. designs for the removal of a particularly nasty and dangerous tyrant from a volatile region may be due to old Europe's resentment of America. "I have been interested to learn," he offers in his piece, "that my hesitation in endorsing war in Iraq is mainly a product of my nostalgia for France's past glory. As Thomas Friedman writes in the *New York Times*, being weak after being power-ful is a terrible thing. Perhaps he is right. I had been deluded into thinking that my doubts about military intervention in Iraq had something to do with fears of civilian casualties, the use of weapons of mass destruction, increasing terrorism or Middle East instability. But apparently we French are really just longing for the time of Napoleon or Louis xiv."

Oh, very droll. The only trouble is, as Sherlock Holmes famously remarked, if one eliminates the impossible, what-ever remains, however improbable, must be the truth. M. Vaisse can't possibly oppose deposing Saddam Hussein for "fears of civilian casualties"—Saddam has been the direct cause of more civilian casualties than anyone in the region—so he must have some other reason. "The use of weapons of mass destruction," or "increasing terrorism," not to mention "Middle East instability," would all be arguments for the removal of Saddam, not against it. Hence, M. Vaisse's prob-lem. Once his proffered reasons are eliminated as impossible, whatever remains, however improbable, is likely to be the truth—even if it's as far-fetched as French nostal-gia for Napoleon and Louis xiv.

But of course one needn't go back to Louis xiv as the sole reason for the stance of President Chirac and his allies. While un inspectors have been scouring Saddam's archives for a paper-trail leading to his weapons of mass destruc-tion, they might with more benefit have been going through French, German, Russian (or even American) archives for the same evidence. Saddam may pose as the defender of Islam these days, but his technology comes from Christendom. The French, the Germans, the Russians didn't need UN inspectors to unearth Saddam's WMD capabilities: They supplied most of it themselves. They're still due some payments from Iraq, in cash as well as in fossil fuel. Collecting from Saddam is as much a French reason for protecting him as nostalgia for the Sun King and his times.

What can't be France's reason is the string of nonsense expounded by M. Vaisse and other Saddamites (as Mark Steyn has called them), to wit: "war would help Osama bin Laden recruit more followers" or "war would trigger more terrorist attacks at home and abroad" or "containment can work" or that "it would be hard to impose stability—let alone democracy—on Iraq, especially when you look at Afghanistan."

This last argument is a winner. Assume Afghan democracy is less than perfect: Would the French favour the Taliban to continue being in charge in Kabul, merrily hosting al Qaeda? Do M. Vaisse and his fellow appeasers actually prefer Mullah Omar and Osama bin Laden to Hamid Karzai?

What makes the French tick? Perhaps it's the curse of Selim Khan III. In 1798, when Napoleon invaded Egypt, the Turkish Sultan proclaimed the French "rebellious infidels and dissident evildoers" and asked God to "debase their banners." The hex half-stuck, it seems to me; ever since the French have had the worst wars and made the best movies about them.

Or maybe the French just have a lot of Gaul. I used to think that Pope Boniface VIII was somewhat intemperate when he remarked, following a lengthy dispute with the French king Philip IV, that he'd rather be a dog than a Frenchman, but after reading M. Vaisse and his fellow apologists, I wonder if the Holy Father was just being practical. After all, having no souls, dogs can't suffer eternal perdition for bearing false witness.

A SEVEN-SIDED VIEW OF IRAQ'S LIBERATION

CanWest News Service, April 3, 2003

Last week the media seemed to concentrate on whether or not the Iraqi people view the U.S.-led coalition forces as friends or foes. Some pundits raised the question genuinely, but most argued for one side or the other according to whether they supported or opposed the war in the first place. Supporters of the war said that ordinary people will greet the coalition as liberators as soon as they're sure the Baathist regime is gone; opponents maintained that most Iraqis will view the Anglo-Americans as invaders.

I think the Iraqis will prove both sides wrong—or both sides right, if you prefer.

Asking whether or not the people of Iraq will look at the coalition as liberators assumes the existence of a unanimity we would never expect to find in a Western country. It's unnecessary to go further than America for an example. In this nation of strong identity and well-developed socio-political values about half the population voted for George W. Bush in the last presidential election, while the other half voted for Al Gore. Considering the ideological gulf between the two candidates, this is an amazing breadth of opinion for a country in which most people share the same liberal-democratic political heritage.

In Iraq, the split would be not only greater, but also more numerous. Even a cursory glance will note a seven-way divide.

First, there will be those Iraqis for whom individual freedom, political democracy, and economic prosperity are important criteria. These Iraqis will no doubt greet the coalition forces as liberators.

Next, there are those who define themselves mainly by their various sectarian or ethnic identities—i.e., people who are Shiites or Kurds before anything else. These Iraqis would, at least initially, consider the forces that removed their Baathist-Sunni oppressors as liberators, though they may not do so for long. For example, many Kurds will not cherish a coalition that prevents them from carving out an independent Kurdistan from Iraq.

The third group of Iraqis define themselves primarily as Arab nationalists. Whether they like and support Saddam or not, they like and support the West even less. They certainly won't think of the coalition as liberators, but as occupiers.

The same is true for a fourth group, who define themselves primarily as Muslim. Whatever they may have thought of Saddam, they won't be happy to be liberated by the infidels. In fact, they'll consider it an insult, if not outright blasphemy. In this context it's worth noting that while Osama bin Laden called Saddam a "socialist infidel" in an audio tape released last year by Aljazeera, he added that it was acceptable for Muslims to fight on behalf of Iraqi "socialists" because "in these circumstances" their interests "intersect in fighting against the Crusaders."

A fifth group of Iraqis actually supported Saddam and benefited from his corrupt and despotic regime. The Baathist officials, the members of "Saddam's fedayeen," the elite cadres of the Republican Guard, will naturally despise the coalition.

A sixth group is the intimidated multitudes. They're regular Iraqi conscripts or civilians afraid of being shot if they welcome, or surrender to, the Anglo-American forces. They include Shiites and Kurds who rebelled after the last Gulf War, only to have their heads chopped off when Saddam was permitted to return. Eventually, these Iraqis will probably greet the coalition as liberators, but not before they're convinced that this time they won't be abandoned to their fate—and who can blame them?

Finally there's a seventh group of Iraqis who know and care about little beyond their daily existence and their families.

They understand next to nothing about democracy. They've accepted Saddam as they had other tyrants and rulers before him, with neither affection nor hostility, as one accepts the weather. While these Iraqis may not be fanatical Arab or Kurd nationalists, or Shiite or Sunni believers, they would certainly regard Westerners as suspicious aliens. For them, the coalition would appear as neither liberators nor oppressors, but as forces of nature, to be outwitted if possible and endured if necessary.

Any estimate about the relative size of these groups would only be a guess, but I think the first group (the outright supporters of democracy and Western values) is probably the smallest, while the seventh group (traditional Iraqis with the least amount of political consciousness) is probably the absolute majority. It's for their soul that Islamists and pan-Arabists will be contending with the West after Saddam and his regime have become history.

THE LIBERAL POSITION

CanWest News Service, April 23, 2003

The liberal position, as expounded by Thomas L. Friedman to PBS's Jim Lehrer this week, is revealing. I'm paraphrasing it here, perhaps somewhat edgily, but I don't think unfairly.

Friedman, a prominent writer and commentator for the *New York Times*, posits that America has friends and antagonists in Iraq, just as in the rest of the Arab/Muslim world.

Our friends are people, whether expatriates or liberated Iraqis, who'd like to see their country develop in democratic and secular ways. Our antagonists are Muslim nationalists who view both democracy and the secular state as alien, unhealthy transplants from the West, to be rejected by the body politic of Islam and the Arab world.

The way to win over our adversaries, in the liberal view, is to forsake our friends.

Friedman's argument is that if we support those Iraqis who prefer democracy and secularism, especially if they're expatriates returning from the West, it will only engender resentment against us. We'll be seen as occupiers or colonizers trying to export our values and influence. The Iraqis we support will seem like our stooges. Whereas if we throw our weight behind the people who represent Muslim and/or Arab nationalism, any theocratic or nationalistic state they establish is less likely to bear us ill will. In time, who knows, such a homegrown Iraqi state may even begin to see the values of democracy and secularism, and develop them indigenously.

Needless to say, the liberal view doesn't counsel us to support militant Islam, such as the more extreme of the ayatollahs, or terrorists like Osama bin Laden, or rejectionists who wish to see Israel replaced by a Palestinian state extending, as their slogan has it, "from the (Jordan) river to the (Mediterranean) sea." No; the liberal point is that we can take the wind out of the sail of such extremists by supporting their more moderate comrades: the ones who don't actually call for jihad and suicide bombers, and are content to peacefully take the prize of Iraq and the rest of the region from the hands of the Great Satan, thank you very much.

For many people—considerations of loyalty apart—deserting a friend in the hope that it might attract an enemy would seem like trading a bird in the hand for one in the bush. But that's not how liberals see it. Liberals find birds in bushes positively irresistible.

As for supporting those who oppose the ideas they stand for, such as democracy and secularism, for liberals this has been par for the course. In fact, it has been the essence of liberal statecraft. Never mind that birds in the bushes often turn out to be snakes in the grass. Fidel Castro was supported by the U.S. in the early stages of his Cuban revolution on the assumption that he was a moderate, non-communist nationalist—in much the same spirit as Friedman now urges America to support moderate Muslim nationalists in Iraq.

In a domestic version of the same syndrome, here's the case of the Philadelphia-based scholar, Daniel Pipes. Dr. Pipes, director of the Middle East Forum and a critic of militant Islam, was recently nominated by U.S. president George W. Bush to serve on the board of the U.S. Institute of Peace (USIP). This aroused the ire of some Muslim activists and apologists for militancy, such as the Council on American-Islamic Relationship (CAIR), who urged the U.S. Senate to reject Pipes' nomination.

Meanwhile, other American Muslims, such as Tashbih Sayyed from the Council for Democracy and Tolerance, along with several Muslim scholars and writers, welcomed the nomination of Pipes. An article in *Pakistan Today* quoted Sayyed as saying that "Pipes scares the Islamists because he has their number," adding that "I agree that Daniel Pipes rattles liberals who value political correctness and tolerance for (likely) terrorists above all else."

As if determined to prove Sayyed's point, an editorial in the *Washington Post* last weekend called for Pipes' nomination to be rescinded on the grounds that it would rub "salt in the wound" of "U.S. Muslims, who are ever anxious that they are being singularly scrutinized."

But who are America's Muslims? Are they the people who reject Dr. Pipes' nomination or those who welcome it? And if they're both, why would America's liberals reflexively choose the first group over the second? The answer, it seems, lies in a basic liberal instinct which calls for America appeasing its adversaries by abandoning its friends.

WHAT NEXT?
National Post, April 29, 2003

Now that the shooting war in Iraq is over, at least for the time being, we can start thinking about the long run—the one of which Lord Keynes famously remarked that we will all be dead in. Still, the long run does permit us one luxury. When turning our eyes to distant horizons, we can do so without hypocrisy, and with all options on the table.

It's easy to be sympathetic to the view—voiced last week by U.S. defense secretary Donald Rumsfeld, even if not in so many words—that the coalition didn't fight a war to depose Saddam Hussein only to anoint some ayatollah in his place. The Bush administration has no wish to stand by while Iraqis substitute some hostile and hideous theocracy for Saddam's hostile and hideous secular regime. Nor did the coalition risk human lives, billions, and considerable political capital to throw Iraq into chaos and possible dissolution.

Yet if the coalition is serious about one of its war aims, also voiced last week, namely that the people of Iraq must decide their own future, it doesn't really matter what future we envisaged for Iraq. Should Iraqis wish to substitute some ayatollah for Saddam, or rupture their fragile federation of ethnic and religious groups, we must remember that we fought a war, at least in part, to enable them to do so.

The Bush administration's vision is of a free Arab society, a first in the Middle East, possibly sparking freedom and democracy throughout the region. Again, it's easy to sympathize. There's an attractive school of thought that puts its trust in the power of freedom. Recently, Nathan Sharansky, once a well-known Soviet dissident, and now Israel's minister of Diaspora affairs, has given expression to it in the *Jerusalem Post*. Mr. Sharansky suggests that "realists" who used to promote détente because they couldn't believe that the march of freedom was inexorable and it would cause the Soviet empire to implode, now feel that Arabs aren't ready for democracy. "Promoting democracy among the Arabs," writes Mr. Sharansky, "is again cast as naive adventurism. The Arabs, we are told, have never lived under democracy. Their culture and religion, we are assured, are inimical to the idea of liberty. The realists dangle the 'pragmatic' alternatives before us: Cut a deal with 'friendly' dictators. They will fight terror. They will preserve order. They will make peace."

Mr. Sharansky argues that the so-called realists are wrong because "the overwhelming power of freedom" will prove as contagious in the Middle East as it was in the Soviet Union. "Soon, Iranians, Saudis, Syrians, Egyptians, Palestinians, and all who live in fear will envy those who no longer do. And they will increasingly find the courage to stand up and say so."

One certainly wishes for Mr. Sharansky's prediction to come true, but meanwhile thousand of Iraqis have been chanting "No to America, No to Saddam, Yes to Islam" during a pilgrimage to the holy city of Karbala. As Daniel Pipes points out in the *New York Post* this week, "'Yes to Islam' in effect means 'Yes to Iranian-style militant Islam.'" Dr. Pipes reasons that, considering that democracy took six centuries to develop in England, we can't expect it to develop overnight in Iraq. For the interim, he recommends "a democratically-minded Iraqi strongman" to hold the country together and keep it from sliding into either anarchy or the lap of a theocratic tyrant. After all, strongmen such as Kemal Atatürk and Chiang Kai-shek paved the way to democracy in Turkey and Taiwan.

One can see Dr. Pipes' point as readily as Mr. Sharansky's. The fact is that when people are free to choose they often make wrong choices—and some wrong choices preclude people from making the right choices later, at least not without another bloody conflict.

What complicates matters further is that we seem committed to the unity of a country whose people may not wish to stay united. It may require a strongman just to prevent Iraq from splitting into its constituent Shia, Sunni, and Kurdish pieces. The question is, what price unity? Why do we, or the Iraqis, benefit from maintaining—possibly as forcefully as Saddam had to—a national construct, artificially created in the 1920s, under a different set of geopolitical circumstances? Why must we oppose, for instance, the emergence of a friendly, democratic Kurdistan, even if it may in time evolve into a Greater Kurdistan carved out of current Iraqi, Iranian, Syrian, and Turkish territories?

An obvious reason is not to upset friendly Turkey—or even unfriendly Iran or Syria—worried about their own Kurdish minorities. But more than our concern for regional stability, we've become so committed to multicultural ideals that we consider all other models of nationhood anathema.

For this we're ready to prop up an artificial entity created eighty years ago that may need a tyrant to function.

But what's sacrosanct about existing countries, in the Mideast or elsewhere, if they lack natural cohesion and need to be held together by force? Why spill blood in the twenty-first century to preserve an entity, such as Iraq, carved out of the Ottoman Empire in the early twentieth century, primarily for the former British Empire's reasons of state? There would be nothing wrong, of course, with such a country, however it came about, if it had internal coherence and viability—but if it can't breathe on its own, why put it on a respirator?

I think our abhorrence of the ethnically (or religiously) based nation-state is a mistake. Worshipping "multicultural-ism" as an overriding concept (i.e., as the only legitimate way for a modern state to be organized) is as erroneous as worshipping tribalism would be. History records many organizing principles. What works, works; what doesn't, doesn't. What's so big about a country that doesn't want to be one?

War is highly focused, which is why the ancients coined their oft-quoted phrase about the law or the Muses falling silent during combat. The silenced Muses include Clio, the Muse of history—but once the din of arms fades, Zeus's daughter begins to speak again. Admittedly, her voice is distant and it's all in Greek, but listening is worth the bother. We'll stumble blindly from war to war unless we decipher her oracles.

INTOLERANCE FOR TERRORISM, NOT FOR ISLAM

CanWest News Service, September 2, 2003

Following the arrest last month of twenty men suspected of belonging to an al Qaeda terrorist sleeper cell, the press quoted Muslim spokespersons saying the charges illustrated Canadian prejudice against Islam.

"It's something against Muslims these days going all around cities," said Ahmad Jaballah, the son of an earlier detainee. "This is racial profiling," offered Tarek Fatah, host of *Muslim Chronicle*, a current-affairs show on CTS Television. A handful of protesters in Toronto carried placards with the same message. "Enough is enough," said Amina Sherazee of the Muslim Canadian Congress.

It was all reminiscent of an item on CNN ten years ago, when a Muslim scholar voiced similar complaints about America.

This was in 1993, after U.S. warships launched a flotilla of cruise missiles at the headquarters of Iraq's intelligence agency in Baghdad. The scholar expressed no support for Saddam Hussein, but still saw the missile raid as evidence of Western intolerance. "It's a double standard," he said. "It's religious prejudice, a hatred against Islam."

The Muslim scholar's wasn't a lone voice. The same year, following the arrest of terrorist suspects, later convicted of bombing the World Trade Center and conspiring to bomb the Lincoln Tunnel and the UN headquarters in New York, a parade of Arab- or Muslim-Americans, introduced as "spokespersons," expressed similar opinions. They used virtually the same terms as the CNN's Muslim scholar. The West was racist or anti-Islam, they said. America displayed religious intolerance and employed a double standard.

Is there any merit in such charges? One way to test the proposition of a "double standard" would be to see what would happen if a Lutheran country—say, Sweden—attempted to assassinate a former U.S. president, as Saddam tried to assassinate Bush, Sr., during a visit to Kuwait. Or if a Catholic religious authority, like the College of Cardinals, started sponsoring terrorist groups to blow up the World Trade Center. If the U.S. protested only by a diplomatic note instead of launching cruise missiles against Stockholm or the Vatican, Muslim spokespersons would be justified in their indignation at the double standard:

"See?" they could say to their CNN interviewers. "When Catholic fundamentalists blow up the World Trade Center the U.S. just looks the other way. And when the prime minister of Sweden tries to assassinate former president George Bush during a visit to Denmark, the U.S. State Department only sends him a note of protest. Poor Saddam Hussein got bombed in Baghdad for the same thing."

But the proposition can't be tested. Catholics, Protestants, Jews, Hindus, and Buddhists adamantly refuse to blow up anything in America these days. Not even the most fundamentalist followers of the other great religions of the world sponsor or encourage assassination attempts against former U.S. presidents or conspiracies to blow up office workers and commuters in New York.

The plain fact is that at the present time only Islamic fundamentalists are engaged in terrorist acts against the West. And as long as this is so, Western responses will only be a measure of our intolerance for terrorism, not of our intolerance for Islam.

Muslims aren't terrorists by definition, of course. Most Muslims by far, whether they live in America or elsewhere, only want to worship God, raise their families, and look after their businesses in peace. It's also true that other religions (and ideologies) have been known to spawn fanatics from time to time.

However, at present, it's only Islamic fundamentalists who have captured the machinery of states that employ terror as a policy. Only Islamic fundamentalists (and Arab nationalists) sponsor terrorist movements worldwide. We don't yet know the identity of the terrorists who blew up UN diplomats and Shiite worshippers in Iraq last week, but it's a fair guess they won't turn out to be militants of the Greek Orthodox Church.

The twenty bogus "students" detained in Canada are young Muslims from Pakistan or India. Contrary to what their apologists assert, that's not what they've been arrested for. Eventually we'll find out whether, as officials suspect, some are part of a terrorist network or have merely engaged in immigration fraud. Either way, they'll be victims of their own actions, not our bias.

It's true that after 9/11, immigration fraud, especially if attempted by young Muslim men, may be suspected of being something worse—but this is prudence, not prejudice. Peaceful Muslims in the West can serve their faith best by sharing, rather than protesting, Western intolerance—not intolerance for Islam, obviously, but for terrorism.

2004

BIOMETRICS AND DISPOSABLE TERRORISTS

National Post, January 18, 2004

The biometric screening of foreign visitors at U.S. airports, announced with much fanfare earlier this month by U.S. security czar Tom Ridge, is a good example of a dilemma peculiar to asymmetric warfare. The more sophisticated the high-tech side becomes, the more it exposes itself to an end-run by the low-tech side.

In a cavern somewhere in the Hindu Kush, Osama bin Laden and his fellow cave-dwellers had come up with a weapon that made biometric screening obsolete before it began. Photo-and-fingerprint machines might thwart old-fashioned terrorists, but in the post-9/11 world the threat comes from another type.

The old terrorist model was reusable; the new one is disposable. The difference is vast. The disposable terrorist is a low-tech answer to the smart bomb. The suicidal militant—

the not-so-smart bomb, perhaps—has a guidance system programmed inside his or her head. He or she is no easier to detect than a stealth bomber and no less reliable than a guided missile. Such terrorists are without a future, obviously—but more importantly, they're without a past.

Civil libertarians object to Governor Ridge's brave new biometrics because they invade people's privacy. For travellers to be photographed and fingerprinted as if they were convicts bound for Devil's Island is irksome and demeaning, but that's the minor problem. The major problem is that travellers are subjected to such indignity for almost no security benefit.

Biometrics target identity, but when militant groups advanced (or regressed) from reusable terrorists to disposable terrorists, identity became moot. Today the acute threat no longer comes from "known" terrorists. Recruits are groomed for a single terrorist act, during which they self-destruct. Before being deployed, disposable terrorists have usually done nothing. They're "innocent" voyagers whose fingerprints and faces appear in no database. And after being deployed, they're just a bloody mist gradually dispersing in the air.

Suicide terrorists consider their lives worthless (no dispute there), but the biometrics of worthless individuals are also worthless. Like bees, disposable terrorists die as they sting—but unlike bees, they cannot be recognized for what they are until they've stung. Machines that compare faces and fingerprints are helpful against reusable terrorists who try to hide their identities, but a disposable terrorist doesn't care if we know who he is.

Until we come up with a machine that can read minds, machines can't help us much. The most sophisticated scanning device is useless if it functions by comparing the present with the past. Disposable terrorists have no past, as a rule; their first act of terrorism is meant to be their last. Biometric machines give us a false sense of security while spreading out the welcome mat to suicide bombers.

This isn't to say that biometric identity checks are entirely useless. They may help identify known organizers of international terror: recruiters, couriers, fundraisers—the office staff. This is a worthwhile function as is the detection of ordinary drug smugglers or embezzlers, but such screens don't remove the acute menace of suicide hijackers flying an aircraft into a skyscraper.

Biometrics are yesterday's solution for today's problem. They can't reduce the threat of the suicide bomber or suicide hijacker on his virgin mission. The contemporary hazard is a terrorist who travels under his own name, his own passport, posing as an innocent student or visitor until the moment he ignites his shoe bomb or pulls out his box cutter.

Identity checks are a good (partial) defence against reusable terrorists. A good (partial) defence against disposable terrorists is a background check. The problem is, unlike identity checks, which can be accomplished in seconds, background checks of any depth take time. If applied to all travellers, they could bring air traffic to a halt. The only way they can be made practical is through profiling.

Profiling has been controversial because, by definition, it discriminates against people of selected ethnicity and religion. Yet we know that disposable terrorists aren't evenly distributed among the world's population. Suicide bombers and suicide hijackers come almost exclusively from certain cultures. Those cultures may shift over historic time, but in a given period they remain remarkably constant. During World War II, kamikaze pilots were Japanese. In our times, disposable terrorists (or warriors) have come from East Asian (Tamil, Sikh) or Arab and/or Muslim cultures. Since Tamil and Sikh terrorists have rarely engaged in suicide action outside their own conflict regions, it leaves people of Arab and/or Muslim background as logical candidates for special scrutiny.

Needless to say, logical as ethnic/religious profiling may be, it's unattractive. It would probably require a second 9/11 for its implementation to become politically feasible.

There is a kind of "profiling" right now, but of the wrong kind. As currently set up, biometric screening isn't applied to all foreigners. Brazilians are subjected to it; Canadians aren't. The problem with this isn't that it's "unfair," as some egalitarians believe, but that it renders the exercise useless. Anyone with a fake identity can avoid biometric scrutiny by travelling with, say, false Canadian rather than false Brazilian papers. Terrorists can simply steal and forge travel documents that belong to one of the twenty-seven countries—say, Britain—whose citizens aren't subject to biometric testing in the U.S.

The shoe bomber Richard Reid, for instance, travelling with a British passport, would have had nothing to fear from biometric screening, even if his papers had been forged, which they weren't. Reid is a perfect example of the new breed of terrorist who would never be eliminated by biometrics—but might be eliminated by profiling. Body-searching young male converts to Islam before letting them board a plane is no doubt discriminatory, but in the case of disposable terrorists like Reid, it could accomplish what biometrics can't.

Even more to the point, today's disposable terrorist doesn't necessarily seek to gain control of an aircraft through the passenger terminal. His preferred route to the flight deck may be through the employment office.

After British Airways Flight 223 was rescheduled for the third time two weeks ago, Brian Doyle, an official with the U.S. Department of Homeland Security, confirmed an earlier report in London's *Daily Mirror*, which quoted an unnamed source about an al Qaeda operative who had supposedly secured employment as a pilot with British Airways and intended to crash the London–Washington flight into the Capitol or the White House. This, apparently, was the reason Flight 223 was once cancelled, once delayed, and once escorted by fighter jets before landing in the U.S. capital this month.

Though this seems to have been a false alarm, there may well be terrorist moles flying or servicing passenger and cargo jets in Western countries, waiting to be activated for a suicide mission. Some may be pilots or flight attendants; others may gain access to restricted places as mechanics, ground crew, baggage handlers, caterers, or cleaners. The papers of such infiltrators are in perfect health; the sickness is in their heads.

Fifth columnists are biometrically correct. They go through airport security, climb aboard aircrafts, and enter cabins or cockpits without subterfuge. It no doubt amuses them to look at passengers shuffling in long lines, waiting to have their photographs and fingerprints taken.

WHO BENEFITS?

National Post, April 4, 2004

Like hyperactive guests on a TV talk show, several topics clamour for attention this week. First in line, though hardly in importance, is Kalle Lasn. He's the editor of *Adbusters*, a left-wing magazine whose March/April issue offers a list of neo-conservative pundits, academics, and government officials Mr. Lasn believes are influential with the Bush administration. The Jews among them are marked with a black dot.

In a piece that goes with the list, Mr. Lasn poses the following question: "Some commentators," he writes (being clearly one of them), "are worried that these individuals—labeled Likudniks, for their links to Israel's right wing Likud party—do not distinguish enough between American and Israeli interests. For example, whose interests were they protecting in pushing for war in Iraq?"

This rhetorical question must seem devastating to Mr. Lasn—a rapier straight through Jewish neo-conservative hearts. In fact, it's rather easy to answer. Considering Saddam Hussein's actual victims, anybody who argued for war to depose his regime was clearly protecting Arab and Muslim interests.

Cui bono?, as lawyers ask, "who benefits?" Throughout Saddam's rule the people he murdered and tortured by the thousands—or millions, counting the years of conflict with Iran—were Iranian Muslims, Kurdish Muslims, Iraqi Shia Muslims, Iraqi Marsh Arabs, Kuwaiti Arab Muslims, and so on. No national group, certainly neither Israelis nor Americans, had as much of a stake in getting rid of Saddam and his killer clan as Arabs and Muslims did. Neo-con Jews protecting Israeli interests? Considering that Saddam's successor may turn out to be a Shiite ayatollah, Mr. Lasn could make out a better case for Irving Kristol, Paul Wolfowitz, Norman Podhoretz, Elliott Abrams, Richard Perle, and the rest protecting the interests of Islam.

Next topic. Citizens of Western-style democracies often find themselves between Charybdis and Scylla (more commonly known these days as a rock and a hard place). On one hand, they have a steady stream of saboteurs, infiltrators, fifth columnists, and agents of influence insinuating themselves in their midst. On the other hand, they're being repeatedly harassed by laws and agencies set up to protect them from such bad guys, but used by the authorities to protect their own posteriors.

When investigative reporters find evidence of official neglect or blunder, the state's response is to go after the reporters. In the days of the old Official Secrets Act the government used security as a pretext for acts of administrative vengeance against their media critics, notably the *Toronto Sun*'s Peter Worthington and the late Doug Creighton. Today's bureaucracy is trying to employ the recent Security of Information Act to the same end against the *Ottawa Citizen*'s Juliet O'Neill. The bureaucrats send out the RCMP in force, as they did twenty years ago, to bluster, intimidate, conduct raids, demand sources, sometimes to trump up charges. The names of the security laws have changed slightly, but the principle remains the same.

One obvious danger is that such heavy-handed tactics might chill reporting. The other is that outrage over police tactics might blind journalists to the acute threat of spies and terrorists. But fifth columnists aren't bogeymen; they do exist. They used to insert themselves into our society and institutions, first as Nazis, then as Communists. Nowadays they appear in their Islamist incarnation. Some prepare acts of terrorism or espionage, and the rest serve as their apologists. They're real, all right—it's just that Canada has two enemies. The first are the fifth columnists themselves; the second are the high-handed, power-hungry, time-serving, mean-spirited, posterior-protecting, obtuse bureaucrats who are supposed to guard us against them.

Quis custodiet ipsos custodes?, as the Romans used to ask, "who is guarding the guards?" On good days, the courts, perhaps; on bad days, not a soul. Oh Canada, we must stand on guard for thee—certainly against thy enemies, but also against thy corrupt and vengeful government, thy pettifogging civil service, and thy self-seeking politicians.

All right; now that I got this off my chest, the next topic. Whenever a Western-style democracy retaliates against a terrorist individual, a terrorist group, or a terrorist state—by an act of war, say, or an act of targeted assassination, such as Israel's recent missile attack on the late Hamas leader, Sheikh Ahmed Yassin—liberal commentators mutter about a cycle of violence and how such acts aren't likely to win the hearts and minds of people who hate us. Liberals have a point. What they don't seem to grasp, though, is that one doesn't shoot one's enemy to arouse his affection, but to kill him.

Which brings me to the final topic. As I'm writing this, the U.S. First Marine Expeditionary Force is preparing to enter the town of Fallujah to settle scores for the murder of four American security guards last Wednesday. "Fallujah is a barrier on the highway to progress," Colonel J.C. Coleman, the Marine's chief of staff, was quoted as saying, sounding understated but rather ominous.

The U.S. civilians were savagely killed and mutilated. I'd be the last person to blame Americans for not letting the matter pass. I only wonder if, after doing what they think they have to do in Fallujah, Secretary of State Colin Powell will still reprimand Israel whenever it responds to atrocities with force.

As Israel's UN ambassador, Dan Gillerman, pointed out last month, the number of Israeli civilians deliberately murdered by Palestinian terrorists as of March 2004 is, in proportion to the country's population, equivalent to 43,136 Americans. "Can there be any doubt as to what your countries would do," asked Ambassador Gillerman, "in the face of terrorism of this scale and magnitude?" When the Marines enter Fallujah, we'll be in a position to hazard a guess.

PAX AMERICANA
National Post, April 15, 2004

There's a demand for Pax Americana and, judging by President Bush's press conference this week, the United States is ready to supply it. The Bush administration seems anything but wobbly. Even so, one wonders if the president and his advisers fully realize what the task entails. To put the genie of anti-civilizational ruthlessness back into its bottle, to defeat terrorist despotism from the nuclear labs of North Korea to the alleys of Fallujah and the caves of al Qaeda in the Hindu Kush, America will need to reconsider decades of ultra-liberalism and political correctness, and revert to earlier models of national purpose.

Specifically, the U.S. will have to:

- Regard any hostile power that attempts to acquire or develop weapons of mass destruction, or refuses to sign and abide by a non-proliferation agreement, as a belligerent state. Such countries must be exposed to the traditional consequences of belligerency, from blockades to possible invasion.

- Acknowledge that, while Islam is a great religion, it contains a strain hostile to Western civilization, and recognize that a state of war exists between that particular strain of Islam and the West. This includes all Arab and/or Muslim countries whose governments nurture or tolerate such a hostile strain.

- Face the fact that terrorism is the chosen tactic of Islamist militants who can't penetrate the defensive perimeters of Western powers from the outside. Face the fact that terrorism depends for its success on fifth columnists; face the fact that Western residents of Arab/Muslim background, along with Arab/Muslim visitors or students, are susceptible to Islamist recruitment as fifth columnists; and face the fact that the loyalty of such residents and visitors cannot be taken for granted. Consequently, much as it may offend liberal and multicultural sensibilities, face the fact that residents, visitors, and, when warranted, even citizens of such background may have to be subjected to profiling, restrictions, surveillance, isolation, and in some cases, expulsion.

- Remember that up to, and including, World War II, military operations weren't conducted with the view that the enemy was merely "the regime" and not the population. The Allies acted on the assumption that the foe was the Germans and the Japanese, even though far from all Germans or Japanese supported the Nazis or the warmongers of Japan. When the Allies bombed Dresden, they didn't try to separate those who voted for Hitler in 1933 from those who voted against him. The imperiums of Wilhelm II or Franz Joseph before World War I, though more liberal than modern dictatorships, were hardly Western-style democracies. They were absolute monarchies whose population might not have endorsed their own rulers in a referendum. Yet it never occurred to the Entente Cordiale to say that it was only fighting the Kaiser and not his subjects. During the Cold War, even though it was evident that most people inside the Soviet camp hated the regime—they brought it down in the end—the West prepared and relied on a nuclear deterrent that by its nature couldn't distinguish between the supporters and opponents of communism.

- Americans will have to consider that making the avoidance of civilian causalities a rigid priority in war has two predictable consequences. First, there's reduced military effectiveness and increased exposure of one's own troops to danger. Second, a campaign may not be evaluated primarily in terms of its military/strategic achievement, but in how successful it was in avoiding collateral damage. This exposes a victorious campaign to the risk of being judged a political debacle if it falls short of some self-imposed goal of minimizing civilian casualties. In short, it increases the likelihood of winning the war and losing the peace. It's ironic when self-imposed Western standards carry such political burden against a terrorist enemy that, far from trying to avoid collateral damage, deliberately targets non-belligerents. Arab/Islamist military efforts specifically express themselves in the bombings (or suicide bombings) of civilian buses, planes, discos, or office buildings, along with *ruses de guerre* such as using civilian shields, dressing military units in civilian clothes, placing military targets in civilian quarters, etc. The indignation of Arab and Islamist belligerents—who, after deliberately targeting civilians, protest when Western or Israeli action results in some collateral civilian damage—ought not to persuade Americans that they have some moral duty to impose extra conditions on themselves in addition to standard conventions of war.

A year ago I wrote that asking whether Iraqis will look at the coalition as liberators is asking the wrong question. It assumes a unanimity in Iraq we would never expect to find in our own countries. In America, most people share the same liberal-democratic heritage, yet even Americans are divided on the question of whether they're liberators or occupiers. In Iraq, there's at least a six-way division. First, there are those Iraqis for whom individual freedom, political democracy, and economic prosperity are important criteria. These people have predictably greeted the coalition forces as liberators. Next are those who define themselves mainly by their various sectarian or ethnic identities. Shiite or Kurdish Iraqis may, initially, have considered the forces that removed their Baathist-Sunni oppressors as liberators, but can hardly be relied on to do so forever, given that the coalition stands in the way of, say, Kurdish dreams of an independent Kurdistan or Shiite dreams of a Tehran-style theocracy. A third group identify themselves as Arab nationalists. Some may have hated Saddam, but like Westerners even less. Ditto for the fourth group, who define themselves primarily as Muslims. They're unlikely to cherish being liberated by the infidels, whatever they may have thought of Saddam. In the fifth group are the "die-hards" currently burning and mutilating Americans in the streets of Fallujah. They actually supported Saddam and benefited from his corrupt and despotic regime. These Iraqis naturally hate the coalition. Finally, there's a sixth group of Iraqis who care about little beyond their daily existence and their families. They understand next to nothing about democracy; they accepted Saddam and his predecessors without either affection or hostility, as one accepts the weather. These Iraqis may not be fanatical nationalists or Muslims, but they certainly regard Westerners as aliens. For them the coalition appears as neither liberator nor oppressor, but as a force of nature, to be outwitted if possible and endured if necessary. Any estimate about the relative size of these groups would only be a guess, but the first group (the supporters of democracy and Western values) is probably the smallest, while the sixth group (the apolitical Iraqis) is probably the largest. It's their souls for which Islamists and pan-Arabists are contending with the West.

Relying on the possibility, or even probability, that most people within Islam—or specifically within Iraq—would prefer to live in a democracy, and that only a minority support despotism and enmity with the West, is a grievous error. It's not an error because it may not be true, but because it's immaterial. Majorities do not necessarily carry the day even in free countries, let alone in theocracies or tyrannies. Militant minorities are far more likely to set the tone in a given country, period, or civilization. Communism was rarely supported by more than 20 per cent of the population in which it held sway. Even a relatively popular totalitarian system, Nazism, was supported only by one out of three voters in Germany's last free election before Hitler assumed power. Western policy makers cannot take comfort in democracy's enemies having only a minority support among their own people. A minority support is all they need. It was all they needed even before the age of terror and weapons of mass destruction, and can do with even smaller numbers in the age of suicide bombers, anthrax, and nuclear devices. It took just nineteen Middle East infiltrators to create the havoc of 9/11 in Manhattan, and about the same for the recent mayhem of 3/11 in Madrid.

Terrorist despotism, theocratic or secular, must be confronted; it cannot be accommodated or appeased. Defeating the enemy is the best way to change his mind. Anti-civilizational ruthlessness, Marxist or Muslim, is to Western democracy what Hannibal's Carthage was to Rome. Some two thousand years ago Marcus Porcius Cato ended his speeches in the senate with the words *carthaginem esse delendam*, "Carthage must be destroyed." At his press conference this week, even if somewhat more diffidently, President Bush conveyed the same message.

THE FUTURE EURABIA

National Post, April 25, 2004

The forecast isn't all grim. There's little doubt that Europe, including Britain, will fundamentally change during the next fifty years. But if it turns into what some commentators are calling "Eurabia," the change won't necessarily mean the end of Western civilization. It need not mean regression to the Dark Ages, the theocratization of secular democracy, or the Islamicization of Christianity. On the contrary, it might bring about the much-needed modernization of Islam.

To know what may happen in Europe and why, it's helpful to recognize what has been happening. Simply put, the Old World has been getting older. Projections show the median age of the countries that currently make up the European Union reaching fifty in fifty years, with about one person in three being sixty-five or over.

These figures come from the United Nations and they factor in immigration. So do the next set of numbers, which show Europe not only aging but shrinking, in absolute as well as relative terms. Currently, the combined headcount of E.U. countries represents about 6 per cent of the world's population, which is down from 14 per cent as the twentieth century began, and on its way to be about 4 per cent by the middle of the twenty-first century. Even in absolute terms there will be about 7.5 million fewer Europeans in 2050 than there are today—and that's with current levels of immigration being maintained.

To be shrinking and aging in a world that's growing and getting younger (the median age in 2002 was 37.8 for Canada, 31.5 for China, 22.9 for Iran, 19.8 for Pakistan, and 15.3 for the Gaza Strip) has some inexorable consequences.

One is that, regardless of how immigrants may change the character of Europe, or whatever backlash they may engender in what the historian Niall Ferguson has called "the economically Neanderthal right," stopping or reversing immigration is no longer an option.

Nativist politicians like Jean-Marie Le Pen in France, the late Pim Fortuyn in Holland, or commentators like Oriana Fallaci* in Italy, may continue to be in the news, increase their following, and even score valid points, but they'll be butting their heads against a demographic stone wall. Even with continuing immigration, Europe's taxpayers can only look forward to their steeply increasing taxes buying them steeply decreasing services. Without immigration, one E.U. taxpayer would soon have to support four or five E.U. pensioners or watch his parents build their last igloo, European-style.

Continuing immigration, though, will likely lead to Eurabia. Immigrants tend to respond to their own demographic pressures, and Europe's fastest growing neighbours today are—to quote Niall Ferguson again—"predominantly if not wholly Muslim." The question is, what will Eurabia lead to?

The past is a good (though not infallible) guide to the future. European nations turned their essentially homogenous countries to U.S.-style immigrant societies after World

---

* Fallaci passed away in 2006.

War II for several reasons, one being the aftermath of empire. The law of unintended consequences caught up with Britain, France, Holland, and Belgium. Their face-saving fictions—such as "commonwealth" or "metropolitan France"—obliged these ex-colonial powers to accommodate a reverse population flow from troubled or depressed regions of their former possessions. The trickle became a flood in the early 1960s as immigrants from North Africa, the Caribbean, or the Spice Islands inundated the home countries, giving politicians like Enoch Powell grey hair.

Another reason applied especially to countries like Germany that needed guest workers as their booming postwar economies quickly outpaced their decimated postwar labour forces. The guest workers' own reason was that European societies—even East European societies, after the Soviet collapse—were more attractive in terms of economic opportunities, social benefits, to say nothing of human securities and freedoms, than the prospective immigrants' native societies.

A final reason, no less important than the others, had to do with changing attitudes. Europeans started accepting immigrants for they had been dazzled by the American melting pot. In the euphoria that followed postwar prosperity, the seeming triumph of rationality and liberal ideals, people in Europe momentarily lost their fear of demographic realities along with many older concerns of the human condition, from scarcity to salvation. Many felt that such ancient quandaries were left buried under the rubble of empire, leaving them free to concentrate on individual self-realization, or new preoccupations from gender equality to the environment.

In practical terms, in addition to welcoming (or at least permitting) newcomers from such unfashionable addresses as Turkey or Algiers, Europeans expressed their new-found spirit of self-confidence by a) going to church less often, and b) having fewer babies. Both activities were replaced by driving more BMWs for longer distances on wider highways and (contradictory as this may seem) organizing more ecological conferences in stylish resorts.

Nature is said to abhor a vacuum. It's hardly surprising that the vacuum left by Europeans in fecundity as well as in religiosity was filled by the Muslim immigrants within four to five decades. In another fifty years mosques may outnumber churches in what by then will be Eurabia—and, more importantly, believers may outnumber unbelievers. While there are more Christians than Muslims in the world—about two billion as opposed to 1.3 billion—nominal Christians far outnumber nominal Muslims.

When only luxury cars increase and multiply in a region, the demographic outcome isn't in doubt. What remains in doubt is what the demographic outcome might mean. Europe Islamicized may resemble the four young British Muslims in David Cohen's "Terror on the Dole," a news story recently published in the *Evening Standard*. The four eat chips with brown sauce while hoping that "Sheikh bin Laden" will bomb London ("I pray for it, I look forward to the day.").

Other British Muslims in the same story dismiss such talk as "verbal diarrhea." Influences work both ways. China was never conquered because it Sinofied immigrants as well as invaders. Will Eurabia be the crucible of Islam's progression from the Middle Ages to the twenty-first century? I don't know, but just asking the question makes me feel better.

THE MUSLIM BOMB

CanWest News Service, June 2, 2004

It's a disturbing thought that terrorists of the most self-righteous and unrelenting kind may only be a heartbeat away from acquiring nuclear weapons. The heart in question belongs to General Pervez Musharraf, and the nuclear weapons belong to Pakistan.

General Musharraf presides over a country that has a high-tech arsenal (small) and a low-tech population (large). Nuclear bombs and donkey carts make for a particularly explosive mixture. The "land of the pure" (the country's name in Urdu) has about half a dozen nuclear warheads to go with 150 million people. Of the latter more than 145 million are Muslims, with a sizeable minority, if not a majority, supporting the Taliban and al Qaeda.

More precisely, the number of Pakistanis who support Islamist militancy are about the same as the number who oppose it. They're both a minority. The majority, as in most parts of the world, is politically inert. Most Pakistanis are simply trying keep body and soul together, and see which way the cat will jump.

President Musharraf and the institutions he controls, from the Pakistani army to the Pakistani media, are firm opponents of militant Islam. Though Muslims themselves, even devout Muslims, they seek development and modernization for Pakistan and accommodation with her neighbours near and far. This is the good news. The bad news is that, although General Musharraf and his circles hold the reins of government, they may be powerless to make the cat jump their way. The country they rule has been variously and accurately described as a "global jihad factory" and a "breeding ground for jihadists."

National Post reporter Stewart Bell, who has quoted both phrases in a recent article, depicts Pakistan as a "terrorist-ridden, nuclear-armed state in an unstable region." One wishes this were an exaggerated or alarmist view, but it isn't. Islamist terror-bombings are commonplace in the country, and there have been attempts on the life of General Musharraf himself. Last week police arrested six members of an al Qaeda–affiliated group, called Harkat-ul-Mujahedin, for an alleged plot to kill the president two years ago. This was only one in a series of plots hatched by fundamentalist forces to remove a leader they regard as an obstacle between their own righteous cause and the Islamic bomb.

The dilemma this poses has no easy answer. It may not have any answer, even a difficult one. It's unfortunate that the development of modern technology in the Third World has coincided with the regression of a great religion, Islam, into medieval militancy and sectarian intolerance. Nevertheless, facts need to be faced. We're dealing with zealots—the kind who'll massacre six members of a Shiite Muslim family, as they did in Lahore recently, including a seven-month-old baby girl, then spray-paint the slogan "Shiites are infidels" on the walls. The possibility that such people may acquire nuclear weapons cannot be contemplated with equanimity, except by fools.

Religious schools—*madrassas*—that manufacture jihadists operate side by side with nuclear labs in Pakistan. Plots by terror organizations such as Harkat-ul-Mujahedin, or Lashkar I Jhangvi (two of whose members attacked a procession of Shiites in Quetta, killing forty-four, before blowing themselves up) or the self-styled Soldiers of the prophet Muhammad, or other like-minded groups mushrooming all over Pakistan, will continue. Even if none ever succeeds in assassinating General Musharraf, illness or old age will remove him from power sooner or later. What then?

The available options are almost equally unappealing. Bomb Pakistan pre-emptively back to the Stone Age? Unthinkable. Remove its nuclear capacity through surgical strikes and by capturing its nuclear scientists? Only in a

Hollywood movie. Change the hearts of its Islamist zealots? In another type of Hollywood movie, perhaps. Make sure that General Musharraf's successor carries on in the same spirit and just as firmly? How can anyone make sure of that?

Doing nothing is the easiest, so that's what we'll most likely do. We'll say, "Let's cross that bridge when we come to it." By the time General Musharraf takes his bow, there will be new twists and turns in the plot anyway. History is improvised, it's *commedia dell'arte*: no script, no prompter, only actors entering, exiting, or waiting in the wings. We invent stage business as the spirit moves us, and say whatever pops into our heads.

Enter a nuclear al Qaeda? Fine, we'll play it by ear. Perhaps we'll rise to the occasion with an inspired line. If not, we can always fall back on a remark by Louis xv: "*Après moi le déluge.*"

ON EXPORTING VALUES

National Post, August 29, 2004

The guns have been silent—well, almost silent—in Iraq's holy city of Najaf in the last four days. Whether or not they'll remain silent (personally, I wouldn't hold my breath) it's instructive to note the reason for the lull in the fighting, temporary as it may be.

The ceasefire didn't come about as a result of any action by Iraq's government. Neither was it achieved by the formidable U.S. forces that have been surrounding Najaf's Imam Ali Shrine these past three weeks. The fighting stopped because an old man returned to the city from London where he was being treated for a cardiac condition.

The Grand Ayatollah Ali al-Sistani, a frail, slow-moving scholar, who looks as if he'd never cracked a smile in his life, accomplished in forty-eight hours what the combined authority and might of the American and Iraqi governments couldn't in months. This fact brings home that when we ship ourselves east of Suez—news from Iraq always conjures up lines from Rudyard Kipling—we enter a different world, with different rules and values.

In a world of different rules and values, waging war is the easy part. Building peace is much harder.

U.S. and Iraqi government forces couldn't budge Shiite militants in three weeks of bloody fighting that devastated sections of Najaf and cost many lives. But almost as soon as al-Sistani arrived, the rebel Shiite cleric Muqtada al-Sadr and his militant followers handed him the keys of the Imam Ali Shrine, then dispersed. This ended the standoff. The U.S. could have, of course, dealt with the insurgents in military terms, except that might have damaged the holy shrine and sparked an upheaval throughout the Muslim world, so it was regarded as a non-starter.

This showed once again that engagement that cannot be fought with all the force that can be brought to bear shouldn't be fought, in most circumstances, at all. Fighting with a hand tied behind one's back isn't likely to gain the moral high ground, but it's almost sure to lose the physical high ground. Al-Sadr and his followers award no Brownie points for restraint, but they can be counted on to take advantage of rectitude. In Najaf, after handing the keys of the shrine to the Grand Ayatollah, the militants dispersed without laying down their arms, contrary to agreement. The U.S. forces dutifully withdrew, as agreed.

In his book, *The Closing of the American Mind*, Allan Bloom described our culture as one of "value relativism." Let's just say that value relativism wasn't the creed of the multitudes that flocked to Najaf from all over Iraq last week. The faithful worshipping the Grand Ayatollah in the streets may have been grubby, hungry, and ill-informed, but they entertained no doubt about good (themselves) and evil (everybody else).

All religions have theocratic impulses; they're capable of existing in fundamentalist or medieval forms, but Islam seems more prone to it than most. The gulf between theocracy and democracy is wide by definition, but in our times it has an extra dimension. We live in a particularly non-judgmental, value-free version of postmodern democracy, while the Muslim world, or at least a good part of it, exists in a highly judgmental and value-laden version of Islamic zealotry. East is East and West is West, as Kipling famously put it, and whether or not the twain shall ever meet, they're certainly not meeting at present.

What are we doing in Najaf? Persuading the Grand Ayatollah, not to mention the ambitious al-Sadr and his fighters, to join the government of Iraq—and to do so on parliamentary terms, genuinely, and not merely as a *ruse de guerre*—has the proverbial snowball's chance in hell. The Shia are 60 per cent of Iraq's population. They've now demonstrated their capabilities. Inspired by their clerics, they can start armed insurrections and they can stop them; they can challenge the central government and they can make truce with it. Shiites are looking for power, not power-sharing.

We (meaning the West) had every reason to overthrow Saddam Hussein's murderous and hostile regime. It's much more doubtful whether we've had any reason to stay in Iraq afterwards. No doubt, we cherish democracy in our own value-free way; even some Iraqis may be attracted to it. But the Muslim world as a whole feels no keener about importing liberal institutions than we'd feel about importing Wahhabism.

Much as we believe in our values, we have to resign ourselves to the fact that, like some wines, values don't necessarily travel. This doesn't remotely mean that we need to isolate ourselves from the world. We can certainly conduct business east of Suez, and we can defend our vital interests. We need to have second thoughts only about nation-building.

If we can resist viewing Western ways as export items, we'll have a chance of avoiding the fool's fate, noted in

Kipling's *The Naulahka*: "And the end of the fight is a tomb-stone white, with the name of the late deceased,/ And the epitaph drear: 'A fool lies here who tried to hustle the East.'"

THE CREDO OF THE JIHADISTS

National Post, September 19, 2004

Chechens started out as freedom fighters, not terrorists. During the 1990s, the struggle for Chechnya's independence engaged the sympathy of many. It had no less a champion than Aleksandr Solzhenitsyn, who came to admire the unbending spirit of the Chechen people he met as a prisoner in Stalin's labour camps.

Solzhenitsyn wrote that "there was one nation which would not give in, would not acquire the mental habits of submission—and not just individual rebels among them, but the whole nation to a man. These were the Chechens." In 1991, then still in American exile, the author of *The Gulag Archipelago* supported independence for most of the Chechen Republic (apart from the historically Cossack lands).

Today, Chechnyan independence is advocated by no Western government and few individuals. By 1999, after militants from Chechnya invaded the Botlikh region of Dagestan, killing eight Russians, Solzhenitsyn himself went on television to voice his conditional support for Moscow's anti-separatist measures in the Caucasus. "For fifteen years we've been withdrawing and capitulating," the eighty-year-old Nobel Peace Prize-winning author said. "We have to stop somewhere."

The French philosopher André Glucksmann, a supporter of the Chechen cause in the West, suggested that the change occurred after 9/11. "After September 11," Glucksmann offered in a 2002 interview, "[Russian president Vladimir] Putin managed to portray the Chechens to the world as terrorists 'working' for Osama bin Laden." In Glucksmann's view, it was Russian disinformation combined with the natural apprehension of the post-9/11 period that caused world opinion to swallow the notion that all Chechens were religious extremists and terrorists. While admitting that "horrible things happened in Chechnya—for example, the notorious murder of the Red Cross doctors," Glucksmann attributed the shift in the world's mood to the success of Russian manipulation and propaganda.

To me it seems the other way around. If world opinion is giving Mr. Putin a hearing today, it's because of 155 dead children in Beslan last week, eighty-nine dead passengers aboard two sabotaged airliners last month, a hundred-plus dead spectators in the Dubrovka Theatre raid in 2002, or thirty-nine people blown up along a parade route in Dagestan five years ago. The Chechen movement for independence, along with other national causes, has been hijacked by the jihadists. Russia may exploit this fact, but it's a fact nevertheless.

Conflicts have been alternately smouldering and raging at Islam's perimeters all over the globe. By 1999, the Islamist leader Shamil Basayev vowed to expel the "infidels" from the North Caucasus. By "infidels," he meant non-Muslims. Before their defeat, Basayev's forces declared themselves to be the government of "Independent Islamic Dagestan." Subsumed into this tide of Muslim militancy, the cause of Chechnya has degenerated into another branch of Islamist terrorism.

A few commentators have been noting this for some time. As David Warren put it last week in these pages, "An independent Chechnya is, notwithstanding the accounts in our media, not the object of this [terrorist] exercise. It is instead to detach Chechnya from the Russian, 'Christian', Dar al-Harb, and attach it instead to the Dar al-Islam—to recover it for Islamdom."

Before the jihadists can take over Dar al-Harb, though, they need to take over Dar al-Islam. They haven't done so yet, but they're making good progress. Xinjiang in northern China is at one end of an Islamic continuum that extends northwest into Kazakhstan, Uzbekistan, the North Caucasus, then southwest into Afghanistan, Pakistan, Iran, Turkey, and ultimately the Middle East. Islamist acts of terror have been recorded in every one of these regions. Uighur separatists in Xinjiang were responsible for some two hundred violent incidents in a decade, according to China.

Who are the jihadists? Paul Verlaine described their possessed type in a poem called "Les Vaincus" (The Vanquished), written after the fall of the Paris Commune in 1871. Verlaine's portrayal of the vanquished Communards would have fit the thirty-two Muslim militants who staged their bloody hostage drama in Beslan, North Ossetia, last week. The echo from Verlaine's stanzas traces the mental landscape of fanatics, religious or secular, historical or contemporary, with the precision of sonar.

The hostage-takers claimed 380 lives in Beslan, almost half of them children. The terrorists refused food and drink for their captives during the standoff. "When children began to faint, they laughed," a hostage named Alla Gadieyeva was quoted as saying afterwards. Verlaine wrote, "*Et nous rirons, sans rien qui trouble notre joie.*" (And we'll laugh with nothing to disturb our joy.) The jihadists behaved just as the French symbolist conjured up the doomed zealots in "The Vanquished."

Verlaine's poem ends with the credo of the fanatics (my translation): "The dogs, the wolves, the birds will peck, claw, and destroy,/ Tear flesh from your bones and dig into your stomachs,/ And we'll laugh with nothing to disturb our joy,/ For the dead are well dead and you learned this lesson from us."

Voices from Dar al-Harb are offering a similarly intransigent lesson. "We showed weakness," Mr. Putin said on Russian television last Saturday, "and weak people are beaten." Once Islam as well as Christendom are taken over by the possessed, a clash of civilizations can't be far behind.

SPEEDING UP HISTORY

CanWest News Service, October 14, 2004

Eleven years ago, in October 1993, eighteen American soldiers perished during a firefight in Mogadishu, Somalia. The tragic loss resulted in much soul-searching about the wisdom and utility of military missions. Many commentators argued on both ends of the political spectrum that America "can't police the world." John Kerry–type politicians muttered darkly about the U.S. being in the wrong war in the wrong place at the wrong time.

I disagreed—just as I disagree with such sentiments today. I wrote that the U.S. should take pride in its initial decision to send the Marines into Somalia. Attempting to feed starving children wasn't some naive, unsophisticated decision. It was nothing to be ashamed of.

In fact, the U.S. succeeded in that mission quite well. The Marines, along with various Western relief organizations, saved multitudes of Somalis from imminent famine. But then something went wrong. The soldiers who went to Somalia to do something soldiers can do, were foolishly kept there to do something soldiers cannot do. This was the mistake.

Is there nothing we can do in the meantime? Oh yes, there is. We can feed children or topple tyrants whenever necessary. If necessary, we can sail in and out of Mogadishu or Baghdad every year. And once we're committed, as we are in Iraq, we can have the fortitude to stay the course.

We can also teach a little and learn a lot. For instance, we can learn to accept that cultures proceed at their own pace. And we can learn to accept that even the most civilized and wealthy nations are powerless to speed up history.

RUNNING THE NUMBERS

CanWest News Service, October 21, 2004

Some math has emerged this week from the facilities at the U.S. naval base in Guantanamo Bay, Cuba. The Pentagon reports that, to date, America released 203 detainees. This appears to be about one out of four prisoners held at "Gitmo," built in early 2002 to intern illegal combatants.

About 540 prisoners are still being detained. Presumably the authorities believe they pose a danger, or haven't yet revealed everything they know (or their interrogators think they know) about the Islamist terror network.

No internee has been tried and convicted. Most haven't even been charged.

Of the 203 released from Guantanamo, fifty-seven weren't set free. They were only transferred into the custody of their native (or citizenship) countries. For five lucky ones this meant Britain; for four further fortunates, France; for another serendipitous soul, Sweden, and for the last propitious pilgrim, Denmark.

Seven unlucky detainees ended up in Russia. You wouldn't want to be an Islamist terrorist suspect in Russia these days. Staying in Guantanamo might be better.

One detainee was sent back to Spain. He might not consider himself lucky either. After the commuter trains were blown up in Madrid, Islamist terrorists were included in the dim view Spaniards had reserved for Basque terrorists until then.

Thirty-eight detainees were transferred to their home authorities in Muslim countries: twenty-nine to Pakistan, five to Morocco, and four to Saudi Arabia. Whether they were lucky or not is hard to say.

The rest of the 203 were determined by the U.S. authorities to either never having been, or no longer being, a terrorist threat. Or so one assumes. They were considered to be neither a danger nor a source of intelligence any longer. They signed a pledge to renounce violence and gained their freedom.

In 139 cases, the authorities appear to have been right. The ex-internees avoided making contact with their former comrades.

In seven cases the authorities were wrong.

A Pentagon spokesman gave scant details this week, but said that one of the seven ended up killing an Afghan judge after his release. Another ex-detainee was described by Pakistani officials as having masterminded the kidnapping of two Chinese engineers, one of whom was murdered. The officials said the suspect's name was Abdullah Mehsud, and he had been released from Guantanamo in March.

Another ex-detainee, named Maulvi Abdul Ghaffar, had once been "a senior Taliban commander in Northern Afghanistan," according to CNN News. Apparently he had spent eight months in Guantanamo Bay, was released, then returned to his homeland to lead a Taliban insurgent force in the south. He was killed on September 26 by Afghan security forces.

A high-ranking U.S. commander in Afghanistan, Major General Eric Olson, has been quoted in a wire service story as saying that "there was no alternative to releasing prisoners from Guantanamo."

"It's not going to be perfect, so it [the Ghaffar case] has not led to any soul-searching about the release program," Major General Olson told Associated Press.

Seven out of 146 isn't bad. The stats look even better if you consider that out of every seven who ostensibly rejoin their comrades at least one may be a double agent. In any event, America isn't China. The world's leading democracy can't hold people in re-education camps forever. Perhaps North Korea wouldn't have a problem with this, but the U.S. ought to—and does.

My concern isn't that seven of 146 ex-detainees relapsed. What concerns me is that twelve ex-detainees came from Western Europe—Britain, France, Sweden, Denmark, Spain—while others held at Guantanamo Bay, or released from it, came from the U.S. and Canada.

What concerns me is that during the war in Afghanistan several young British Muslims volunteered to fight for the Taliban and against their own country. When two of them, Afzal Munir and Aftab Manzoor, both twenty-five, from Luton, Bedfordshire, were reported killed in Kabul, Muslim communities expressed sympathy for the volunteers. The BBC quoted Ajmol Masroor of the Islamic Society of Britain saying that, "With the current policy of attacking innocent Afghanis, I think we're alienating a vast majority of second generation Muslims."

Most Muslims and/or Arabs who live in Western countries aren't terrorists. Even sympathizers and apologists are a minority. But the needs of terrorism are frugal. Only nineteen suicidal attackers, armed with box cutters, can down four airliners, demolish two of the world's largest structures, and kill three thousand people.

Nineteen equals three thousand. Of all the math emerging from Guantanamo Bay, that's the equation that worries me.

DEMOCRATS FOR THEOCRACY

National Post, November 22, 2004

The debate isn't new, but it has flared up in recent weeks. Can Western-style democracy be brought to Islamic countries? If so, can it be imposed from the top down, whether indigenously as Kemal Atatürk tried in Turkey three-quarters of a century ago, or by outside influence, as President George W. Bush is trying now in Iraq? Or must it evolve through a gradual change in traditional Islamic institutions?

In the current issue of *Washington Monthly*, Michael Hirsh suggests that the fallacy of imposable democracy can be laid at the door of historian Bernard Lewis. According to Mr. Hirsh, the renowned Princeton scholar's "Kemalist vision of a secularized, Westernized Arab democracy" has taken hold of the imagination of the policy makers of the Bush administration. Other Middle Eastern scholars "have quietly stewed over Lewis's outsized influence." To critics such as Columbia's Richard Bulliet it comes as no surprise that "Lewis and his acolytes in Washington botched the war on terror."

It would be a mistake, I think, to dismiss the debate as a mere turf war between academics. Nor is it just a side product of America's own culture wars between the left and the right. Though writers like Mr. Hirsh—a senior editor of *Newsweek*—or scholars such as Professor Bulliet are considerably left of Professor Lewis, I don't think this alone defines their arguments.

There are people on both sides of the left-right divide who take it for granted that Western-style democracy and modernity would benefit Islamic nations, coupled with the belief that it's possible for Islamic nations to achieve democracy and modernity. There are also people on both sides who aren't convinced of the first proposition, and seem downright skeptical about the second.

Idealists consider democracy desirable and irresistible. Realists consider it desirable but resistible. About eighteen months ago Nathan Sharansky, once a well-known Soviet dissident and later an Israeli cabinet minister, argued in the *Jerusalem Post* that realists are wrong: Even though Arabs have never lived under democracy "the overwhelming power of freedom" will prove as contagious in the Middle East as it was in the Soviet Union.

"Soon, Iranians, Saudis, Syrians, Egyptians, Palestinians," Mr. Sharansky wrote in 2003, "and all who live in fear will envy those who no longer do. And they will increasingly find the courage to stand up and say so."

Today it seems that in the Arab/Islamic world it's those who don't like freedom (as we understand the word) who are increasingly finding the courage to stand up and say so. Some people in these countries put their lives on the line for democracy, but many seem to prefer some form of tyranny. The scholar who had it right in 2003 may have been Daniel Pipes, who recommended "a democratically minded Iraqi strongman" to keep the country from sliding into either anarchy or the lap of a theocratic tyrant.

"Democratically minded strongman" sounds like a contradiction in terms—reminiscent of a 1960s Turkish law that provided two years of imprisonment for anyone who publicly stated that Turkey wasn't a democracy. Though this seemed like joke out of Monty Python, it wasn't; it was applied Kemalism. Atatürk, who died in 1938, did modernize Turkey, just as strongman Chang Kai-shek did pave the way to democracy in Taiwan.

Force isn't inimical to democracy. As Amir Taheri put it in the *New York Post* last week, "A measure of military force may be needed, not to impose democracy, but to remove impediments to democratization."

Leftist critics consider the idea of strongmen spearheading democratization a "Lewisian-Kemalistic" fallacy. Mr. Hirsh spells this out then implies that it's also a Western-style imperialist fallacy. He snarkily refers to Iraq's interim prime minister Iyad Allawi as "our man in Baghdad." Here's the left's memo to the White House: forget democracy. The choice in Iraq is between extremists like Abu Musab al-Zarqawi and moderates like the Grand Ayatollah Ali al-Sistani.

In this view, the White House should arouse itself from dreams of Western-style political systems in Arab/Muslim lands. The West created "corrupt, kleptocratic tyrannies" following World War 1 then imposed Israel on the region following World War II. These are injuries and insults the Arab/Islamic world won't forget. In the foreseeable future, Arabs and Muslims will either choose "moderate" theocracies like Iran, or extreme ones like the Taliban.

Islamic democracy may evolve—by unspecified means—from Iranian-type theocracies. Such democracies will have the merit of civilizational continuity. Until they appear, all the West can do is make conciliatory noises and send foreign aid. The left's second memo to the White House reads: a) you can't export values, and b) you've nothing of value to export anyway, except perhaps feminism.

There are people on the right who might agree with a). None would agree with b). Those who agreed with a) would do so regretfully. In contrast, the left appears to anticipate a world of "moderate" ayatollahs armed with nuclear weapons with equanimity, if not enthusiasm.

Mr. Hirsh and Professor Bulliet would no doubt describe themselves as democrats rather than theocrats, yet seem to favour moderate theocracy over moderate democracy in the Middle East. Observers may consider this a non sequitur. I think it is—though not inconsistent with the left's other conclusions that fail to follow their own premises.

GOING DUTCH

CanWest News Service, November 24, 2004

A liberal friend said to me at dinner this week, "If there's one subject I almost feel like a conservative about these days, it's immigration."

My friend is a filmmaker. He's not as left-leaning as Michael Moore, but close. "You should go to Holland," I advised him. "You'd feel right at home."

If a neo-con is a liberal who has been mugged by reality, Holland is rapidly filling with neo-cons. More precisely, it's filling with people whose desire to protect liberal ideals compels them to take a conservative stance on one: immigration.

It ought to have been predictable. The Netherlands, as Arnaud de Borchgrave put it in the *New York Post* last week, "has long been Europe's most permissive society." The same permissiveness that made Amsterdam the hookers-and-hashish capital of the world tended to encourage immigration with little regard to the host country's economic or cultural needs.

Europe's immigrants come primarily from Muslim countries; in Holland's case, mainly from its former colony in Indonesia. Today, the tiny Dutch kingdom finds itself with an undigested blob of about a million Muslim immigrants congregating chiefly in its four largest cities. They tend not to blend into the host country's culture but live, in de Borchgrave's words, "among themselves, with their own schools, mosques and restaurants."

Ironically, but not surprisingly, what some immigrants have come to dislike about Holland is the very spirit of ultra-liberalism that enabled them to live there in the first place. And the permissiveness—indeed, licentiousness—of Dutch society offends those Muslims most who aren't culturally acclimatized to tolerate what they consider offensive.

The concentration of a sizeable bloc of people intolerant of liberal shibboleths has begun to ring alarm bells in the minds of Dutch liberals who see a threat to their own values. Unlike France or Belgium, where unbridled immigration is usually opposed by right-wing politicians like Jean-Marie Le Pen or the Flemish Bloc party (recently disbanded), in Holland opposition comes from people like the late homosexual politician, Pim Fortuyn, and his supporters. Though the media often described Fortuyn and his party as "far right," they were anything but. When the flamboyant sociology professor founded Lijst Pim Fortuyn (Pim Fortuyn List), it was to protect liberal notions, such as tolerance for gays, from the religious intolerance of Muslim immigrants.

After Fortuyn was murdered by an animal rights crusader in 2002, his concerns continued to be voiced by other liberals. They included Theo van Gogh, a grandnephew of the painter, who made provocative and pornographic films about what he considered the ill-treatment of women in

Muslim societies. On November 2, van Gogh was murdered by a man who pinned a note to his victim's chest calling on Muslims to rise against the Western infidel. Reports describe the prime suspect as Muhammad Bouyeri, a twenty-six-year-old Dutch Moroccan.

Last week, a popular politician in the Netherlands called for a five-year moratorium on immigration. The media identify Geert Wilders as a right winger but this, too, comes from force of habit. In fact, the Groep Wilders (Group Wilders) is a splinter from Holland's Liberal Party, its former coalition partner. Groep Wilders has now taken up the banner of Lijst Pim Fortuyn in parliament.

"We are a Dutch democratic society. We have our own norms and values," Wilders was quoted as saying in a recent interview. "If you chose radical Islam you can leave, and if you don't leave voluntarily then we will send you away."

If Dutch liberals have started sounding like the late Enoch Powell used to sound in Britain during the 1960s, there's a reason. "The Netherlands has been too tolerant to intolerant people for too long," was the way Wilders put in his interview. It would be hard to put it better.

Super-liberalism has sub-liberal consequences. Admitting immigrants from distant cultures in numbers greater than host countries can comfortably assimilate creates a problem even when host countries and immigrants both make an effort at cultural integration. The problem becomes worse when American-style "melting pot" and even

Canadian-style "cultural mosaic" models are abandoned for ultra-liberal models of "multiculturalism" and "diversity."

That's when European Union officials hastily agree, as they have at a recent conference of E.U. justice and interior ministers, "to demand that new immigrants learn the language of their adopted countries and adhere to 'European values'." Trouble is, by then immigrants have turned into invaders and natives into vigilantes; some nutcases have murdered politicians, while others have burned mosques. And some Canadian liberals, like my filmmaker friend, are going Dutch.

2005

REAL MUSLIMS AND FALSE MUSLIMS

National Post, July 11, 2005

The interviewer was asking about the terrorists. "They aren't Muslims," replied the distraught man, clutching a photograph. Behind him, an older man nodded. "They aren't even human."

The two men in the NBC news clip wore traditional Bangladeshi clothes. A caption identified one as Shamsul. They were being interviewed in a Muslim-populated area of London, near the station where one of the bombs went off. Both looked unprepossessing, but the snapshot one held up to the camera showed a young woman of surprising beauty. "Daughter," the man identified as Shamsul said, tapping the photo with his finger for emphasis. Apparently she was still missing, thirty-six hours after the explosion.

The older man was the woman's grandfather. "I used to hold her, like this..." he explained, as if an accurate demonstration of how he held his granddaughter twenty years ago might aid in her recovery. The father was still responding to the earlier question. "They can say, who did this, that they're Muslims," he repeated, "but they're not."

The camera lingered on his face as he desperately waited for confirmation from someone, anyone, that the terrorists didn't share his faith. There was none forthcoming. In his white tunic, wearing fez-shaped headgear, Shamsul looked like a person in denial. Or like someone who had just suffered a devastating triple loss, robbed in an instant of his daughter, his religion, and his reputation.

Shamsul seemed to anticipate that the people who "did this" in London will call themselves Muslim, just as the people who did Madrid on March 11, 2004, or the people who did New York and Washington on September 11, 2001, called themselves Muslim. When he said, "they aren't Muslim" he meant that terrorists who blow up trains or fly passenger jets into office towers may claim, or even think, they're acting for Islam, but they aren't. People who act for Islam are like Shamsul. They work hard, raise sturdy sons and beautiful daughters, and believe that God is merciful and killing is wrong. Real Muslims blow up nothing. On the contrary: real Muslims, or their beautiful children, risk getting blown up themselves when they travel in planes, trains, or buses targeted by false Muslims.

It's impossible not to sympathize with a man who, in the space of a few minutes on an ordinary Thursday morning, not only loses a precious child to a savage band of barbarians, but his religion as well. After claiming the life of his daughter, the feral assassins claim Shamsul's spiritual life by reducing his Islam, a complex and compassionate faith of mercy and tolerance, to a primitive and brutal creed of fanaticism, malice, and mayhem. And then, adding a final insult to injury, his neighbours in the heart of Europe, instead of recognizing a fellow victim, may look at him with fear, loathing, and suspicion because he shares, even if only nominally, the religion of his daughter's murderers, possibly along with their garb, voice, appearance, and gestures.

It would be comforting to agree with the distraught Shamsul that he alone is the real Muslim, and the terrorists aren't. But the unhappy truth is that they're both real. In the House of Islam there are many rooms. Pretending that those who blow up things aren't real Muslims may postpone waking up to harsh reality, but sleeping through a war isn't a viable option. And we *are* at war: At war with a branch of Islam.

We're not at war with "terrorism." Terrorism is a weapon, not an opponent. We've been at war with militant, fundamentalist Islam that uses terrorism as a weapon.

Of course, militant Islam has been at war with Shamsul's moderate Islam as well. Shamsul's is the bigger war. Muslim victims of Muslim violence dwarf non-Muslim victims. The first number in the millions (counting Bangladesh, Saddam's depredations against Kurds and Shiites, the

Iran-Iraqi war, etc.). Non-Muslim fatalities barely add up to twenty thousand, even after decades of low-grade global terrorism, Kashmir, Chechnya, two Gulf wars, and 9/11.

There have been three main strands of violence running through the Arab/Muslim world since World War II, two secular and one religious. One was quasi-Marxist and resulted in such terrorist organizations as George Habash's Popular Front for the Liberation of Palestine, founded in 1967. The PFLP engaged in some spectacular hijacking operations throughout the 1970s. The other secular strand was Arab national-socialistic, spawning such Nasserite and Baathist regimes as Colonel Gaddafi's in Libya, the al-Assad-family's in Syria, and Saddam Hussein's in Iraq. As for Yasser Arafat's PLO, it straddled—some say, bridged—the Marxist and national-socialistic shores of the pan-Arab stream, alternately quarrelling with, and borrowing from, both sides.

Terrorism was part of Marxist and pan-Arab nationalism, but the worst violence emerged from Islam's religious revival. Initially encouraged by the West to counteract Marxist influence, militant Islam grew in the hothouses of Wahhabi oil sheiks, the *madrassas* of Pakistan, the CIA-sponsored training camps of Afghanistan, and the revolutionary councils of theocratic Iran. Eventually, it resulted in al Qaeda, as mobile, intangible, and destructive as fire.

The malevolent flame followed Shamsul to London. He needs our help to put it out. We need Shamsul's.

A DEMON RIDING ON THE BACK OF A GOD

National Post, August 2, 2005

Osman Hussain, captured last week in Italy, is talking. That's the good news. The twenty-seven-year-old terrorism suspect reportedly claims his failed fellow London bombers of July 21 had nothing to do with the deadly London bombers of July 7. That's the bad news. If true, it indicates that the world faces a bigger problem than a conspiracy of fanatics such as al Qaeda. We're facing a malevolent spirit that spontaneously generates fanatical conspirators.

When Muslim suicide bombers blow up commuters in London and vacationers in Sharm el-Sheikh, it's not the easiest thing to remember that Islam is a religion of peace. Yet one must try to remember it.

"The face of terror is not the true faith of Islam," remarked U.S. president George W. Bush while visiting a mosque shortly after 9/11. The war with terrorism is in many ways "an inter-Islamic struggle," added University of Toronto professor Clifford Orwin around the same time. Such statements are hard to swallow while picking up body parts from the rubble, but the president and the professor are right. Islam has many faiths, many struggles, and many faces.

Radicalized Muslims equate true Islam with conquering Islam. They look to Islam's "base"—which is what "al Qaeda" means—rather than to the zenith of Islam's civilization. They feel nostalgia for Islam's sword rather than for Islam's architecture, poetry, or mathematics. They find their inspiration in the tribal savagery of Islam's desert beginnings rather than in the prosperity and tolerance of Islam's urbane maturity; in the romance of the conquest of Mecca rather than in the sagacity of the great Caliph of Córdoba, the times of Abd-ar-Rahman III.

In other words, radicals feel nostalgic for Islam's vices rather than its virtues. And some radicals live in the West.

They're few in number. Western Muslim communities have chosen modernity and democracy, on the whole. Most immigrants from Middle East countries voted with their feet for freedom versus tyranny, enlightenment versus the Middle Ages. But while moderates easily outnumber militants, they don't necessarily outweigh them. Active minorities are more adept at setting the tone and agenda of a community than passive majorities.

Good news: about two out of three Muslims living in the U.K. say they would report Islamist terrorists to the police. Bad news: it follows that about one in three wouldn't. Good news: hardly any Muslims would actually commit a terrorist act. Bad news: hardly any are needed. Terror isn't labour-intensive. Just nineteen terrorists brought down three passenger planes and murdered nearly three thousand people on September 11, 2001. There are 1.5 million Muslims in Great Britain. Osama bin Laden needs only one in eighty thousand to stage another 9/11.

Islamism equals a demon hitching a ride on the back of a god. Why does Islam tolerate it?

David Frum has quoted the Canadian Muslim writer Irshad Manji—author of the book *The Trouble with Islam*—writing in the *Wall Street Journal*. "[U]nlike Judaism and unlike Christianity," Manji suggests, "the spiritual elements of Islam are mixed with an ideology of war and conquest, even in the pages of the Koran itself."

Frum has this comment: "You often hear people say that the Islamic world needs Reformation. Alas, in many ways, Islamic extremism is the Muslim Reformation. Al Qaeda and its ideological supporters are rejecting a thousand years of interpretation—interpretation that has tended to soften the often harsh Koranic text—to return to the bald words of Islamic scripture."

Ottawa Citizen columnist David Warren characterized Osama bin Laden's message as "the need for war, the final war, between the decadent West, and an aroused Islam with a billion soldiers." All of Islam certainly doesn't agree with bin Laden. The fraction that does, though, makes up in intensity for what it lacks in numbers.

"We are sure of our victory against the Americans and the Jews as promised by the Prophet," bin Laden explained to John Miller of *Esquire* magazine in February 1999.

"Judgment day shall not come until the Muslim fights the Jew, where the Jew will hide behind trees and stones, and the tree and the stone will speak and say, 'Muslim, behind me is a Jew. Come and kill him.'"

Muslims who oppose bin Laden and the terrorist branch of Islam rarely speak with such force and clarity. This has changed a little since 7/7, and there have been exceptions even before. In 2004, for instance, The Middle East Media Research Institute (MEMRI) quoted a Syrian academic, Mundir Badr Haloum, writing in the Lebanese daily *Al-Safir*.

"Ignominious terrorism exists," Professor Haloum wrote, "and one cannot but acknowledge its being Islamic. Islam is in need of true reform. Islam's need [for reform]— or, to be precise, our need for Islam's reform—is not less than the need for reform in the Arab political regimes. This is the need for people who are capable of fearlessly acknowledging that terrorism nests within us as Muslims and that we must exorcise it."

The columnist John O'Sullivan wrote once that Nazism and Communism were malformed offshoots of Western civilization, not something apart from it. One could argue that since Islamism is Islam's malformed kin, Islam itself will have to destroy it, just as the West had destroyed its own monstrous progenies.

Exporting democracy is also an attractive idea. President Bush is certainly betting the farm on it. But as an antidote to Islamofascism, democracy might be counterproductive in some Muslim countries. The autocrats of Pakistan or Saudi Arabia are relatively better disposed towards Western values than many of their people. Genuine democracy in such countries may only be a prelude to an Islamist takeover.

I'm an optimist in the long run. The short run looks grim. Things are likely to get better, but not before they get a good deal worse. So foul a sky, as Shakespeare observed, clears not without a storm.

HISTORY HAS YET TO JUDGE 9/11
CanWest News Service, September 15, 2005

My flying partner, David Frid, was at the controls of our single-engine four-seater on September 11, 2001, when Toronto Radar declared the airspace over North America closed, requesting all civilian aircraft to land immediately at the nearest suitable airport. In his twenty-plus years as an airline pilot, Captain Frid had never heard such a request. The first thought flashing through his mind was of war. Frid landed at Muskoka, Ontario, suspecting a nuclear attack or accident, and half-expecting to see a mushroom cloud rise in some quadrant of the brilliantly blue sky.

So did other cockpit crews in this hemisphere.

No one knew what happened for the first few hours. Did the flight crews of Flights AA11, AA77, and UA 175 obey hijackers and crash their jetliners into New York's Twin Towers and the Pentagon in Washington? Frid doubted it. He didn't think that an air transport pilot could be ordered to crash into a building. Flying into a structure would entail certain death anyway, so pilots would resist. It seemed much more likely that the hijackers of Flights 11, 77, and 175 incapacitated the flight crews before crashing the planes into the World Trade Center and the Pentagon.

By noon it was time for me to file a column. I speculated that some of the terrorists must have had at least rudimentary training as pilots. "Flying a sophisticated airliner any distance requires a degree of skill, even if the person at the controls wishes only to crash," I wrote a few hours after the Twin Towers came down. "A Boeing 757 or 767, the type of aircrafts involved in yesterday's outrage, cannot be steered into a target building by someone who has never flown before."

The terrorists had flown before, as it turned out. They had gone to flight schools in America. They acquired a constructive skill in our culture, mixed it with their own culture, and turned it into a destructive skill.

And therein lies a puzzle. Al Qaeda's terrorists claim to act in the name of Islam, yet Islam isn't a culture of death. If it were, a billion human beings wouldn't thrive under it around the globe. Cultures of death are self-limiting, but Islam is defined by its birth-rate, not its suicide bombers.

But is there something else about Islam that is conducive

to the formation of extremist sects? Is Islam a petri dish nourishing a culture of radical fundamentalism?

Arguably, yes. Some creeds are friendlier to the separation between a social and a spiritual realm than others. The idea of a separate Church and State predates the U.S. constitution. It's rooted in Christianity, where it's expressed as rendering unto Caesar the things that are Caesar's and unto God the things that are God's. This notion is absent in Islam. For Muslims, all things belong to God, including the State. Separation amounts to sacrilege.

Such a civilization may discern any manifestation of modernity an assault on its beliefs. If some secular values— say, equality for women—contradict some tenets of the faith, not being able to separate the things that are Caesar's (or civil society's) from the things that are God's, is more likely to invite a radical response.

All religions have, or have had, radical phases. All religions contain passages of darkness and light in their holy books. However, while militant fundamentalism is dormant in all religions, in our day it appears to be awake in one.

If so, is our diverse and tolerant society merely an antebellum illusion? Is 9/11, like Sarajevo or Pearl Harbor, a divider of epochs, the herald of a world conflagration?

As heralds, Sarajevo and Pearl Harbor were similar. As causes, they weren't. Sarajevo might have remained a localized outrage if the response of the great powers, coupled with the public mood, hadn't turned the assassination of

Archduke Franz Ferdinand and his wife into a *casus belli* for a world war. But Pearl Harbor couldn't have been undone with restraint alone. After Pearl Harbor it would have been impossible, or at least very difficult, for "sober heads to prevail." A Serb nationalist's sneak attack on a Habsburg crown prince and his wife didn't make the First World War inevitable; the Japanese Imperial Navy's sneak attack on the American Republic's Pacific Fleet made the United States' entry into the Second World War a foregone conclusion.

Will 9/11 prove to be closer to Pearl Harbor or to Sarajevo? On the fourth anniversary, it's still too early to tell.

OF HORSES AND WATER

CanWest News Service, December 1, 2005

Speaking at the Grano Speaker Series in Toronto last week, British-American journalist Christopher Hitchens defended George W. Bush's jihad to install democracy in the Middle East. Hitchens suggested the U.S. president's struggle was far from being futile or wrong. After all, in a country where "just three years ago, possessing a satellite dish would invite death," today there's a parliament, six TV channels, and twenty-one newspapers.

Sure, someone might retort, six TV channels, twenty-one newspapers—and a civil war. What price TV channels and satellite dishes? Is Iraq's new-found access to a cacophony of voices trying to drown out one another worth dozens of people being blown to smithereens every day?

This argument currently divides the Western world. The Bush White House, Tony Blair's 10 Downing Street, Christopher Hitchens, and a steadily diminishing number of ordinary citizens are on one side, while the mainstream media, the *New York Times*, the *Washington Post*, the *Guardian*, the BBC, the CBC, and about 70 per cent of American, British, and Canadian public opinion are on the other. They believe Bush is minimally wrong, if not evil.

Detractors of what they call "Bush's war" ask how a squabbling parliament in Iraq, propped up by American bayonets, can possibly be called democracy? How is the bloody circus of Saddam's trial, with defence attorneys intimidated and assassinated, anything like the rule of law? Some critics of the war, like former U.S. national security adviser Brent Scowcroft, think that it was wise to leave the Baathist dictator in power at the end of the First Gulf War in 1991. The people of Iraq were actually better off under Saddam.

And if the Iraqi people were better off, why on earth did Bush have to depose Saddam by force? We now know that he never had weapons of mass destruction. What did we gain? If we let Bush depose other Baathist-style despots, like the Assads of Syria, we will only hazard upsetting (in Scowcroft's words) "fifty years of peace."

Supporters of Bush's jihad for democracy tear their hair out when they hear such arguments. They ask (as Hitchens did in his speech last week) how anyone could "possibly say the last half-century was a period of peace?" What about the invasion of Kuwait? What about the Kurdish genocide? What about a million dead in the Iran-Iraq War?

Inevitably, both sides in the debate end up with sweeping pronouncements on the political culture of the Arab/Muslim world. Essentially, the verdict is either "they're just like us" or it's "they're different." The side that favours Bush's policies considers democracy self-evidently superior to other political systems, and takes it for granted that most people in the world, including the world of Islam, seek and desire it. Those who oppose Bush's policies aren't so sure. They feel that democracy may be an alien flower in the Middle East. They may question the universally beneficial nature of democracy, or its support among Arabs and Muslims, or both.

Which side is right, or at least closer to being right? I find it revealing that in the early phase of the war, while Bush appeared to be winning, his support was at about the same 70 per cent as his opposition is today. Which—surprise, surprise—indicates that questions of right and wrong often resolve themselves into questions of success and failure. Politicians become statesmen by winning the wars they launch. How? Often by knowing when to quit.

As in gambling, winning means quitting while one is ahead. If Bush the president had remembered what Bush the candidate so often repeated on the campaign trail—no nation building—his war against Iraq's tyrant would have ended in a rapid and undisputed victory. If after removing Saddam from his rat hole, the U.S.-led coalition had considered its mission accomplished and withdrawn, it wouldn't have lost most of its maimed and dead and, along with them, much of its fighting spirit. As for Iraq, it would have been free to build its own nation and democracy.

Impossible, many argue. American withdrawal would have meant civil war in Iraq, not democracy. Perhaps so, but what's happening in Iraq now is civil war anyway—except it's civil war under American supervision and with American casualties.

It seems evident that many people want democracy in the Arab/Muslim world. America can clear a path to democracy by toppling tyrants. Deposing dictators is like leading a horse to water. It isn't a mistake. The mistake is trying to make it drink.

2006

BOVINES AMONG THE CROCKERY VERSUS APPLE-POLISHERS OF APPEASEMENT

CanWest News Service, February 9, 2006

Combative secularists have the edge. They can trigger a clash of civilizations more easily by printing crude drawings of the prophet Muhammad in Denmark than militant Muslims can by murdering commuters in Madrid or London. There were no outbreaks of anti-Muslim riots in Europe following the massacre of passengers on Spanish trains and British buses, but enraged mobs burned European embassies in the Middle East after the appearance of a dozen cartoons in a Danish newspaper.

Christendom—or rather post-Christendom—tolerates actual injury better than Islam tolerates perceived insult. Whether or not this state of affairs will last is hard to tell. Present trends are unlikely to continue, for if they did, secular Europe would surrender to theocratic Islam without a fight. I don't think that's in the cards.

Some European newspaper reacted to dire Muslim threats against Denmark by printing drawings of the Prophet themselves. In response, Muslim riots around the globe intensified. In Beirut a gunman shouted, *"Allah akbar!"* (God is great!) before shooting and killing a Catholic priest.

It's a safe bet that Father Andrea Santoro had nothing to do with the cartoons in the Jyllands-Posten. On the contrary, chances are he'd have disapproved of them. Offending people in their faith for a lark, as the Danish newspaper may have done, is adolescent and uncouth.

But there are worse things than being childish and ill-bred—shooting people, for one. Murder is against the teachings of most religions—including, presumably, Islam's, although from the behaviour of some Muslims these days it's difficult to tell what is or isn't against the teaching of Islam.

Choosing sides in a debate where the tone is set by rambunctious numbskulls is no easier. Blaspheming God's messengers to provoke simple folk with chips on their shoulders is sophomoric: so much for one side. Being thin-skinned and self-righteous enough to be provoked by witless cartoons is moronic: So much for the other. The clash of civilizations is shaping up as a rumble between the morons and sophomores of this world.

It's one thing to cherish and defend freedoms, and quite another to assert them in the manner of a bull in a china shop. Exercising freedoms merely to hurt and annoy people is at best juvenile. Often it's also mean-spirited. It serves only to provide the commissars of the interventionist state, who dislike and fear freedoms anyway, with an excuse for curtailing them.

As bad as bovines among the crockery are the apple-polishers of appeasement. They respond to everything by self-censorship, a.k.a. political correctness. These hybrids between mice and men elevate their cowardice into a pretence of maturity. They market surrender under the label of adult wisdom, as if scurrying into the nearest hole made anyone look grown-up.

The U.S. scholar Daniel Pipes has news for this group: "The key issue at stake in the battle over the twelve Danish cartoons of the Muslim prophet Muhammad," he writes in the *New York Sun*, "is this: Will the West stand up for its customs and mores, including freedom of speech, or will Muslims impose their way of life on the West? Ultimately, there is no compromise: Westerners will either retain their civilization, including the right to insult and blaspheme, or not."

The conservative commentator, John O'Sullivan, makes the further point that "contrary to much 'responsible' commentary, *Jyllands-Posten*, the small regional Danish newspaper that first published the caricatures of

Mohammed, did not do so from trivial motives. This was not the kind of avant-garde 'shock' tactics on show in 'Piss Christ' or in the 'Sensations' exhibition in Brooklyn that included a painting of the Virgin Mary splattered with elephant dung. It was a serious and justified protest against the fact that Danish artists had been frightened out of illustrating a children's book on Islam and Mohammed."

One thing detracts from the force of these attractive arguments. The values they urge Western civilization to defend against Muslim medievalism have been surrendered to the liberal-fascist state long ago. Our freedoms of conscience and expression, including the right to blaspheme and vituperate, have long been confiscated by the thought-police of "progressive" left-liberalism (a.k.a. human rights commissions). The wrong word about immigration, gender, matrimony, or history can land anyone in the dungeons of IUP-FEMEGD, the Inquisition Upholding the Primacy of Feminist-Environmentalist-Multiculturalist-Egalitarian-Gay-Dogma.

It's a toss-up between questioning a shibboleth of feminism and drawing a caricature of Muhammad: Ask Harvard president Lawrence Summers. No wonder the rioters of Islam accuse the West of hypocrisy.

MESSAGE FROM THE MAD: LEAVE THE SAINTS ALONE

National Post, February 17, 2006

The news photo showed a mob torching a building in Beirut. The rioters were objecting to the notorious Danish cartoons of the prophet Muhammad. An acquaintance was looking at the picture in utter bewilderment.

"Are these people mad?" he asked me.

It was a logical question. Sane people in my acquaintance's neck of the woods would rarely set fire to buildings for any reason—and if they did, it would have to be a reason infinitely more tangible and proximate than a cartoon published in a faraway country, offending religious sensibilities.

"No, they're not mad," I said. "They're just differently sane. They're sane in a manner suitable to their own times."

"What do you mean, their own times? Muslims live in the twenty-first century, the same as you and I."

My acquaintance was half-right, which can be worse than being entirely wrong. True, contemporary Muslims have an address in the twenty-first century. Some use it most of the time; some commute between it and their other address in the twelfth century, while others live mainly in the twelfth century and maintain a twenty-first-century address for email.

The jets that leave western airports for Asia and the Middle East double as time machines. They transport travellers back to the Middle Ages, a period when burning down things for blasphemy or sacrilege was an eminently sane thing to do.

A drawing of Muhammad, blasphemy? Surely that in itself is crazy. No, not in the twelfth century. The creation of "craven images," along with the pictorial representation of divine or saintly figures, used to be highly controversial in Christendom as well. We find faint cultural echoes of this doctrinal dispute even in relatively recent works, such as Puccini's opera *Tosca*. When the painter Cavaradossi is decorating the ceiling of Sant'Andrea della Valle with a fresco of Magdalene, singing his famous air "Recondita Armonia," the church's arch-conservative sacristan keeps punctuating the artist's sublime paean to beauty with a recurring grumble, "*Scherza coi fanti e lascia stare i santi*" (Have fun with servants but leave the saints alone.)

By the Napoleonic era, when Puccini's opera takes place, the sacristan could only grumble. A few centuries earlier, though, the same dispute might have resulted in a St. Bartholomew night, a massacre of the Huguenots, the sacristan's sect of Christians burning Cavaradossi's sect of Christians at the stake (or vice versa). Islam extended this medieval attitude to our own times. The militants are courteously holding up a mirror for us in post-Christendom to see our own twelfth-century faces.

But, of course, there's more to it than that. Ours is also the age of the Arab/Islamic awakening. If there's method in

Islam's revolutionary madness, there's also madness in its revolutionary method—a deliberate, cultivated madness. The poet Nizar Qabbani gives perfect expression to it in his great ode to the intifada, a panegyric to the "children of the stones."

O mad people of Gaza,
as thousand greetings to the mad
The age of political reason
has long departed
so teach us madness

In other words, don't mess with us, we're crazy. We'll throw stones at armoured vehicles, strap on suicide bombs, respond to cartoons with riots. We're irresistible because we've nothing to lose, because our kingdom is not of this world, because we cherish death more than you, our enemies who cherish life.

How did the Arab/Islamic awakening reach this point? Like the great Oriental/Asiatic awakenings at the turn of the twentieth century, it began by measuring itself against the high-achieving, prosperous, arrogant, seemingly invincible West. Then Arab/Islamic and Oriental/Asiatic routes diverged. The big Far Eastern and Asian powers of Japan, China, Russia, and India, tried to lick the West. They ended up essentially joining it when licking it proved to be too difficult. The Arab/Islamic world tried initially the other route, and resolved to lick the West only because they couldn't join it.

It's a Shakespearean tragedy in three parts.

Act I. During the twentieth century the Arab-Turkish-Persian world keeps taking wrong turns on the road to Westernization. It chooses blind alleys of fascist-style nationalism and quasi-Marxist socialism. The result is the Suez crisis, the Six Day War, the First Gulf War.

Act 2. Far from catching up to the West, the former lands of the Ottomans and the Moguls fall even farther behind. This suggests to the next generation that the route to Arab/Islamic renaissance leads through fundamental Islam.

Act 3. Exeunt Colonel Gamel Nasser, Dr. George Habash, Yasser Arafat, and Saddam Hussein. Trumpets. Enter the Ayatollah Khomeini, followed by al Qaeda.

WILL WE BECOME CANARABIA?

National Post, March 31, 2006

A poet friend in Europe, who prefers to remain anonymous, sends me this postcard from Florence, Italy. (The English translation is my own.)

> In European politics
>   people play for keeps.
> What a bigger power sows,
>   a smaller power reaps.

Lawrence of Arabia's dead.
Ah, but never mind,
in Florence of Eurabia
his legacy's left behind.

A few day later, looking at a copy of Oriana Fallaci's *The Force of Reason*, I come across this paragraph: "In 1978, I remember it well, they were already occupying the Historical Centre of Florence. 'But when did they get here?!?' I asked the tobacconist of piazza Republica where they assembled with particular delight. He spread his arms and sighed: 'God knows. One morning I woke up and here they were.'"

The Force of Reason, hot off the press, is the second of the fiery Italian journalist's book-length pamphlets that have been creating a publishing sensation in Europe. (The first volume, *The Rage and the Pride*, published in 2002, had sixteen printings in two years.) The "they" in the passage quoted refers to the Arab and/or Muslim immigrants who have turned Italy's (and Christendom's) historic city into the "Florence of Eurabia" in my anonymous poet friend's postcard.

On the other side of the Atlantic, writing about a recent demonstration of illegal immigrants protesting a proposed U.S. law that would sanction employers who hire undocumented workers, the columnist John O'Sullivan offers this description: "The demonstrators occupied the public square in their thousands. Though asked by the politically cautious organizers to bring along only American flags, half the flags they waved were Mexican. They brandished placards and shouted slogans accusing the United States of stealing their land."

Just a snapshot maybe, but not a pretty picture. It bears no resemblance to those beaming faces of multicultural harmony in citizenship brochures.

Arab or Hispanic, legal or illegal, in North America or in Europe, the last thirty years have marked the emergence of a new kind of immigrant. He isn't new to history, strictly speaking, only to his immediate predecessors. He's unlike the immigrant types to whom he bears a superficial resemblance: the explorer-adventurer, the refugee, the exile, the asylum-seeker, the settler, the pioneer.

The new immigrant is none of these, though he may share one or another of their attributes. The new immigrant is an invader.

The invader-immigrant appears in times of fundamental population shifts, the Great Migrations of history. Such migrations occur from time to time. They did, for instance, between the third and the fifth centuries, and they appear to have started again in the twentieth. Just as the invader-migrants of other historic periods could be of any tribe—Visi- or Ostrogoth, Hun, Gepid, Lombard, Avar, to name a few—the invader-migrants of our times may be Asian or Levantine or Caucasian. They may be Muslim or

Sikh or Christian or anything else. Invasion as a concept isn't race- or religion-specific, though it's usually tied to specific groups and cultures at specific points in time.

Whatever their background, the new kind of immigrant doesn't simply compete with the host population for jobs, economic opportunity, and space (all of which can be shared) but for identity, which cannot. Immigrants can and do create jobs, as well as compete for them, making the score even. But immigrants can't create identities for the host population; only compete for the existing identity of a nation.

This makes certain "small" matters, often dismissed as merely symbolic—permitting turbans on construction sites, say, or ceremonial daggers in schools—actually more important than ostensibly hard-nosed economic issues between immigrant and host communities. They can be more divisive for being demanded as well as for being denied—and they can be especially divisive for being granted.

A flag—a piece of fabric on a stick—is just a symbol, but a demonstration in America conducted under an American flag is materially different from one conducted under the flag of Mexico. The first is a country trying to share a problem; the second is a problem trying to share a country.

A country like Canada can share its space, resources, job opportunities, and wealth with newcomers more easily than Italy, but it cannot share, let alone give up, its identity anymore than Italy could. Toronto may be an immigrant city in a way Florence isn't, but "Canarabia" is no closer to Canada than Eurabia is to Europe. If we fail to keep this in mind, one night we'll go to sleep in a familiar place and wake up next morning, feeling as helplessly puzzled as Fallaci's tobacconist in the piazza Republica.

GUARDIANS OF THE TRUTH
CanWest News Service, April 6, 2006

The modern liberal state has its dogmas and taboos. It guards and enforces them almost as rigidly as Iran's revolutionary tribunals enforce their version of Islam. Canada still has a distance to go before it becomes anything like Iran, but it's edging closer to a kind of secular theocracy, genuflecting to political correctness, a long way from the free country it once used to be.

Ironically, the march towards the new dark ages started with the introduction of human rights legislation some thirty years ago. By now the human rights commissions have become our Iran-style revolutionary tribunals. In Canada, we've ways of dealing with people who think they've a constitutional guarantee of free expression. As Muslim activists haven't failed to notice, the way around the Charter leads through a thicket called human rights.

The Islamic Supreme Council of Canada—yes, that's what it's called—has recently requested the Alberta Human

Rights Commission to deal with the *Western Standard* for its editorial decision to re-print some Danish cartoons featuring the prophet Muhammad. For readers who have had better things to do than keep up with the minutiae of Muslim sensitivities, last fall a newspaper in Denmark published a series of cartoons of Muhammad. This sent Muslim mobs, incited by their mullahs, on murderous rampages in various parts of the globe. The riots having made the cartoons a legitimate news story, some papers, including Ezra Levant's *Western Standard*, decided to re-print them so people could judge for themselves what the bloody fuss was all about.

If Syed Soharwardy, president of the Islamic Supreme Council of Canada, felt offended by the *Western Standard*'s exercise of its editorial discretion, he had an excellent remedy, available to any person in a free country. He could say so. He could denounce Levant's decision in speeches, in print, in letters to the editor, in peaceful protest marches or in public meetings. He could persuade Canadians—or try to—that reprinting the Danish cartoons was somehow wrong.

But Soharwardy and colleagues, in line with the authoritarian nature of their creed, preferred a top-down solution. They tried persuading no one except the authorities. Believing that disagreeing with them ought to be a police matter, they started with the Crown's office. Then, when told that running a cartoon of the prophet Muhammad wasn't a criminal offence in Canada, at least not yet, they went to the human rights commission.

I suppose Alberta's Muslim leaders could have done worse. Like imams in other places, they could have tried inciting riots. To their credit, they made no attempt to do so. But neither did they consider that in a secular democracy people trade freely in a marketplace of ideas, opinions, and beliefs. Instead of debating Levant, they first tried to have him arrested, then turned to our society's nearest kin to theocratic repression, the holy inquisition of the shibboleths of super-liberalism, the politburo of Canada's multiculturalist-collectivist-feminist-environmentalist axis, where they struck gold. The Orwellian commissars of Alberta's human rights directorate, instead of advising Soharwardy and company to go soak their heads in cold water, started processing their complaint.

Can anything good come from such a "human rights" complaint? Can a pressure group's assault on fundamental freedoms make this country a better place? Yes, perhaps. Soharwardy's attack may, just may, cause Canadians to finally re-examine the concept of human rights commissions.

Even a chief architect of the concept, Alan Borovoy, general counsel of the Canadian Civil Liberties Association, is beginning to notice the hideous chickens coming home to roost in his barnyard. "During the years when my colleagues and I were labouring to create such commissions," he wrote last month in the *Calgary Herald*, "we never imagined that they might ultimately be used against freedom of speech."

Borovoy should have imagined it, partly because it was self-evident, and partly because I told him so during our discussions of the subject some twenty years ago. We argued about it nearly every Saturday in the late 1980s, sitting with friends in a Toronto café. It seemed to me then, as it seems to me now, that Borovoy's crowd of left-leaning liberals could imagine all right how the "human rights" laws they promoted could be used against somebody else's freedom of speech—some conservative fuddy-duddy's, for instance. What Borovoy's brand of "progressive" cosmopolitans couldn't imagine was that their laws might one day be used by conservative fuddy-duddies—even veritable clerical-fascist imams—against their own freedom of speech.

Well, hallelujah. The day is here.

HEZBOLLAH REAPING THE WHIRLWIND IN ISRAELI CONFLICT
CanWest Publications, July 20, 2006

The Arab/Muslim side in the Middle East conflict follows what has become a three-step formula. One, sow the wind. Two, reap the whirlwind. Three, complain about the weather.

Amazingly, much of the world listens.

The facts in this latest round are straightforward. On Wednesday, July 12, Hezbollah, an Iranian and Syrian-backed terrorist organization operating in southern Lebanon, unleashed a sudden and totally unprovoked attack into Israeli territory. Scores of Katyusha rockets rained down on such Israeli towns and villages as Nahariya, Zefat, Rosh Pina, and the port city of Haifa. As Israel's UN ambassador, Dan Gillerman, reported to an emergency session of the Security Council, in a period of forty-eight hours more than five hundred Katyushas and mortar shells were fired into the northern part of Israel. Initially they killed two civilians and wounded hundreds more, including many women and children. And while this barrage was going on, Hezbollah terrorists infiltrated Israel across the Lebanese border. They killed eight soldiers and captured two more, taking their captives deep into Lebanon.

I don't think that "sowing the wind" is too strong a term to describe such an action. There's no country on earth that wouldn't react to an assault of this kind with military measures if it had the capacity to do so. React, that is, not necessarily in retaliation, but in defence. Whether a thrust like Hezbollah's should or shouldn't go unpunished may be debatable; what is beyond debate is that it can't go unparried, and the only way to parry rocket and artillery thrusts is to destroy the batteries and launch pads from which they're fired.

In the words of Ambassador Gillerman, "Israel had no choice but to react, as would any other responsible democratic government. Having shown unparalleled restraint for six years while bearing the brunt of countless attacks, Israel had to respond to this absolutely unprovoked assault whose scale and depth was unprecedented in recent years."

Which brings us to the issue of proportionality. Granted that Israel "had to respond," as its ambassador put it, did it have to respond so strongly? Did it have to respond with a massive bombardment of Lebanon's infrastructure? Did it have to attack such seemingly non-military targets as roads, airports, apartment buildings, villages, inevitably causing civilian casualties?

There are long answers, but the short answer is: you bet.

Proportionality is smuggled into the moral debate mainly by those who worry about the consequences of their misdeeds, and look for insurance that no matter what they do, even if it's to deliberately fire rockets at civilians, they'll only suffer so much punishment for it. Proportionality certainly isn't the biblical injunction against misdeeds. The Lord didn't say, Sow the wind and you'll reap a proportionate wind. He said, Sow the wind and you'll reap the whirlwind. Hezbollah, being ostensibly men of God, ought to know this.

God's injunction aside, proportionality is a bizarre demand in any but a sporting contest. If taken literally, it would call for modern armies to scrap their smart bombs and fight with nothing except weapons and tactics available to Saddam and Slobodan. Such rules of engagement would have the coalition forces still battling Iraq's Republican

Guards with Soviet-era tanks. Even more importantly, such a requirement would reward the most cynical ruses and deceptions, putting the side that is trying to observe the Geneva conventions at a disadvantage.

If a party used ambulances to transport ammunition, and as a consequence the other party started firing at ambulances, which party would be in breach of the Geneva conventions? This isn't an abstract question. Hezbollah and Hamas routinely employ such deceptions, then cry crocodile tears if Israel refuses to fall for them. As Ambassador Gillerman put it in the UN, "Many of the long-range missiles that have hit Israeli towns were launched from private homes with families residing inside, where a special room was designated as a launching pad, with the family playing host to the missile."

Terrorists use Arab families as human shields to launch rockets from their homes at Israeli families. They regard it as a win-win proposition: if Israel worries about collateral damage, Hezbollah's launch pads are safe, and if Israel rejects this kind of moral blackmail, the terrorists create more "martyrs" and score more points in the propaganda war.

It worked in the past, but this time Israel seems willing to let Hezbollah win the propaganda war. What it won't let Hezbollah win is the war. Watch for the whirlwind.

CANADA'S ARBOUR IS PORTIA TO ISRAEL'S SHYLOCK

CanWest Publications, July 27, 2006

Eureka! I've stumbled upon the secret of the countries Israel has never bombed or invaded. Different as they may be from one another, they have one thing in common. These countries have never bombed or invaded Israel. Nor have they funded, sheltered, armed or incited any group to do so.

They haven't even made menacing gestures while developing weapons of mass destruction, like the former president and current star hunger-striker of Iraq, Saddam Hussein.

The phenomenon is consistent enough to be reduced to a simple formula. I'll offer it here as Jonas's Law: To avoid being bombed and invaded by Israel, avoid bombing and invading it first.

Avoid also funding, sheltering, and supplying terrorists, on your own soil or elsewhere. Avoid inciting proxies to infiltrate, shell, booby-trap, sabotage, kidnap, or otherwise expose to physical harm Israeli installations and residents. To be on the safe side, don't even threaten to destroy Israel at some future date. Don't, especially, combine veiled threats with a nuclear development program, like President Ahmadinejad of Iran. If you can resist doing this, the historic record guarantees you a bomb- and invasion-free existence as Israel's neighbour.

It's not necessary to like Israel. Whether you are a fanatic mullah, a pan-Arab nationalist, or just an ordinary Arab or Muslim, whether you get on well with the People of the Covenant or consider them the sons of pigs and dogs, you don't have to fear military measures until you start throwing things at Israelis first—and I don't mean stones. Stones invite rubber bullets in response; you need to throw rockets to invite the Air Force. No matter how much you detest Israelites in particular or Jews in general, as long as you can content yourself with calling on God's wrath to rain down on the Jewish State, and refrain from reinforcing your prayer by supplying missiles to Hezbollah, you can exercise your religious freedom of loathing with no other consequence than perhaps being loathed in return.

It seems necessary to jot this down because current critics of Israel, before they start muttering darkly about war crimes, tend to preface their remarks with the pious bromide, "Of course, Israel has a right to defend itself."

That's good news for Israel—or would be, if the people who say so meant it—for Israel never did anything but defend itself from attack, actual or impending. A country whose sole war aim is to exist is defensive rather than aggressive by definition. The Jewish State's internal monologue, like Hamlet's, has always been "to be or not to be." You don't look for a fight, if all victory can achieve for you is the status quo. No one bets his house on the proposition that if he wins, he can keep it.

Look at what a belligerent can hope from victory, and you'll see whether he's defensive or aggressive. This simple test demonstrates that all of Israel's wars have been defensive since 1948. If the world truly accepted that Israel had a right to defend itself, there could be no criticism of its actions, no moral issues, and no talk of war crimes even when innocent civilians get hurt. But Israel's "right to defend itself," to which its Western critics are careful to pay lip service, hinges on Israel never actually doing so.

The Jewish State is entitled to armed self-defence; it just cannot shed any blood.

If this sounds familiar, it may be because it's straight out of *The Merchant of Venice*. Shakespeare's heroine, Portia, disguised as a doctor at law, tells the duke that the Jew Shylock has a valid contract. If the Venetian merchant Antonio cannot honour his bond, Shylock is entitled to a pound of his flesh and can use a knife to obtain it. But, says Portia, the contract says nothing about blood. Shylock taking a pound of flesh is a legitimate creditor, but if he draws as much as a drop of blood, he's a criminal.

Gotcha!

The play was popular then—a smart lawyer sticking it to the avaricious Jew, all perfectly legal—and it's popular today. The UN plays the duke; Israel is cast as Shylock, and Lebanon as Antonio. Canada contributes a contemporary Portia to lay down the law. Oh yes, Israel can defend itself against a camouflaged Hezbollah hiding among the civilian population, but if it sheds any civilian blood, it commits a war crime. Please welcome Madame Justice Louise Arbour.

JIHADISTS DON'T CARE ABOUT LOGIC
National Post, September 23, 2006

To counter any suggestion that Islam is a violent religion, Muslims attacked churches in the West Bank, Gaza, and Basra this week. In Somalia a religious leader named Abubukar Hassan Malin echoed a British religious leader named Anjem Choudary who seemed to be in agreement with a religious leader from India called Syed Ahmed Bukhari that Pope Benedict XVI had to be forced to apologize.

Forced? Bukhari left it open how, but Choudary felt that subjecting the Pontiff to "capital punishment" may be persuasive, while Malin was inclined to think that the situation called for hunting down the Holy Father and killing him "on the spot." And, perhaps to indicate that these were no idle threats, as the week wore on, an Italian nun was murdered in Somalia, along with two Assyrian Christians in Iraq.

What did the pope do? As most readers know, he quoted a remark made by the Byzantine emperor Manuel II Palaeologus: "Show me just what Muhammad brought that was new, and there you will find things only evil and inhuman, such as his command to spread by the sword the faith he preached."

Was the anointed of Byzantium on to something? The pope certainly didn't say so. He just quoted the beleaguered emperor, who—being squeezed between hostile Turks and demanding Venetians at the time—had vented about the Prophet and his bellicose followers in conversation with a Persian scholar. Little did he suspect that his words would hit the fan nearly six hundred years later.

"The infidelity and tyranny of the Pope will only be stopped by a major attack," announced al Qaeda from its cave on the Afghan-Pakistani border. Al Qaeda's political arm in New York, a.k.a. the United Nations, took no position, only using the opportunity to condemn Israel for one thing or another.

Why do some Muslims have such an uncanny talent for proving the case of their critics? When accused of violence, they threaten violence. Better still, they engage in it. "Call us unruly and we riot," they say, in essence. "Call us murderers, and we kill you." Don't they see that this makes them a joke?

Well, no, they don't—and they're right. Saying such things may make someone a joke in a debating society, but Islamofascists fight in a different arena. They don't care about winning the debate; what they want to win is their *kampf*, better known these days as jihad.

Lo and behold, they're winning it. By now the whole world tiptoes around the sensibilities of medieval fanatics.

We take pains not to offend ululating fossils who cheer suicide bombers. Or raise them. We prop up rickety regimes whose sole contribution to modern times is to nurture ancient grievances and revive barbaric customs. We worry about the feelings—feelings!—of people who stone their loved ones for sexual missteps. We pussyfoot to protect the delicate psyche of oily ogres who amputate the hands of petty thieves, issue fatwas on novelists, and cover up their hapless wives and sisters to the eyeballs.

We do this, obviously, not because we're impressed by the logic of the Islamofascist line—"call us murderers and we'll kill you"—but because we're intimidated by it. The jihadists don't care about the quality of their argument. One doesn't have to, if one's aim isn't to persuade, but to coerce. The mullahs of militant Islam aren't worried about proving their critics' case. So some pundits think we're proving Benedict XVI or Manuel II right, imams Choudary and Malin might say. Big deal. Logic may be essential for pundits. It isn't essential for our followers who are willing to blow themselves up to get their way.

Come again, slowly—blow themselves up to get their way? Yes, sir. How's that for logic?

The sheiks and mullahs of conquering Islam don't give a hoot about the hearts and minds of the West (the place that used to be called Christendom). They figure, not without justification, that if they get us by the balls, our hearts and minds will follow. This phrase, by the way, usually attributed to John Wayne, is a rare example of successful cross-pollination between the West and the East. It comes from cowboy country, but even Taliban-types understand it.

We're fortunate, though. To grab us by the balls, the Islamofascists would first have to find them. Good luck.

Last question: did the pope apologize for upsetting the mobs so the poor things had to vandalize and murder? Well, that depends on what *sono rammaricato* means in English. The Vatican seems to think it means "I am deeply sorry," but some commentators swear it only means "I am disappointed." Personally, I'd be disappointed if it meant "I am deeply sorry"—but that's only me.

POSTSCRIPT: THE WOUNDED STORK

Schoolboys in my native Hungary used to recite an old ditty. It conjured up emotions ossified in the seams of time.

> Stork, stork, *ciconia*,
> What makes your foot bleed?
> A Turkish lad is slashing it
> A Magyar lad is mending it
> With a fife, a drum, and a fiddle of reed.

The wounded stork's song was a fragment of tribal memory bobbing to the surface from the collective unconscious of a great historic hurt. It was a bitter lay, a denunciation of the Ottoman Empire, the Xanadu of imperial Islam. The Turks had occupied Hungary for six generations. Although the 150 years of Turkish rule occurred during the sixteenth and seventeenth centuries, the Magyars never quite got over it.

The national bird's lament was a manifestation of recollected trauma, but as the words cast a spell of their own, on the playground we repeated them oblivious to their overtones of ethnic and civilizational hostility. Apart from the puzzle of how to mend a bleeding foot with musical instruments, we were enticed by the alliteration of the first line. It rendered the Latin word for "stork"—*ciconia*—as *gilice* in Hungarian, to harmonize with the Hungarian word for "stork"—*gólya*—and made the first line go: "*Gólya, gólya, gilice.*" Mournfully pronounced as "goh-yah, goh-yah, ghi-lih-tzeh," the words burrowed into our minds. The fiddle of reed (no one knew what a fiddle of reed was, but it sounded magical) was icing on the cake.

The melodious ditty would be viewed as offensive to "diversity" today. We meant to give no offence to anyone— none of us had ever seen a Turkish lad—but we did associate the song with what we had been told about the Turkish occupation of Hungary—the Turkish *hódoltság* or "bondage," as we invariably referred to it, just as Palestinians refer to the creation of Israel as *nakba*, or "catastrophe."

Being in thrall to the Turk meant being in thrall to Islam. This was worse than being in thrall to the German— Hungary's other great historic trauma—for Germans were at least kin in Christ, while Turks were Muslims.

Christianity's roots in Hungary were not very deep, but they did go back to the ninth century (with pagan revolts extending into the eleventh). The Magyars, a coalition of seven tribes of nomadic horsemen from Siberia, kept riding west until they emerged from familiar Asia and found themselves in alien Europe. This happened shortly before the end of the first millennium. The Magyar chieftains concluded that they had no choice but to adopt Christianity and settle in the fertile lands along both banks of the river Danube, in a region the Romans had called Pannonia.

The chieftains did not realize that they had picked a natural conflict zone. They pitched their tents in the borderlands between civilizations. Buda Castle was still a long way from being built in 895 AD, but the grey Danube (it was never blue) roiling at the foot of the future seat of Hungary's kings was the last in a series of moats between East and West, Asia and Europe, paganism and monotheism. In due course, it became a moat between Islam and Christendom.

Having made the mistake of settling in a bad geopolitical neighbourhood, the Magyars would come to see themselves as defenders of the West, to which they did not belong, against the East, to which they did. This resulted in Hungarians having a love-hate relationship with both the East and the West for the next thousand years. "East" meant Mongolian and Tartar marauders at first, but the expansion of the Ottoman Empire during the fifteenth century gradually changed its meaning to include Islam. The crescent moon became a symbol of menace, as the Muslim world made up for the ground it lost in southwestern Europe by its conquests in the southeast. By victories such as Kosovo, the Prophet's armies gained in the Balkans what they forfeited in Spain. Eventually, their success saw them sweep across the great plains of Hungary and Transdanubia, their high tide reaching the walls of Vienna on two occasions, the last time in 1683.

The Magyars resisted Islam's advance for nearly a century, but eventually they succumbed at Mohács Field in 1526. After that debacle, Hungary's 150 years of bondage began. Ottoman rule was not unmitigated evil—for instance, horticulture and architecture flourished under it—but it was still a nightmare of caprice and corruption. The Sultan's soldiers were fatalistic in combat and merciless in victory. The Porta—Turkish court—combined dizzying hauteur with abject servility. It also combined, along with its entire culture, Oriental cruelty with Muslim self-righteousness. Most measures were considered justified against the *giaours* ("infidels"). The trauma of imperial Islam lingers in the lower Danube-basin to this day.

I am offering this potted history of the region because my reader is likely to be the product of what I have called "the sixty-year gap." Assuming that he or she was born after 1918 (the year General Allenby rode through the gates of Damascus) but before 1979 (when the Ayatollah Khomeini deposed the Shah of Iran and the mujahadeen began resisting the Soviet Union in Afghanistan) my reader belongs to only about three generations in 1,400 years during which the struggle between the Islamic and non-Islamic world was on standby. This sixty-year gap between the collapse of the Ottoman Empire and the resurgence of militant Islam was one of the few periods in which people, as long as they lived in certain sheltered parts of the world, such as Western Europe and North America, could be blissfully unaware that their civilization was at war with another.

Even this sixty-year gap was a matter of perception rather than reality. The struggle never abated. Pakistan and India conducted full-scale engagements, as did Israel and the so-called rejectionist Arab states surrounding it. Still, in the Western perception—and in the Arab perception as well to some extent—the struggle in those years was between the forces of Arab "national liberation" and Western "imperialism" rather than between the armies of the Prophet and those of the infidels.

The illusion of a gap in the ancient struggle lasted three generations and had certain consequences. One was that when the smouldering fire of Islam's jihad erupted again in 1979, it caught many, if not most, Westerners by surprise. The fourteen-century-old conflagration was burning brightly, with American hostages being paraded in Tehran, but many people took another twenty-two years to notice the flames. Millions did, finally, on a picture-perfect

September morning in 2001, though others denied seeing the fire even then.

Some still deny it.

Having grown up in the land of the bloodied stork, I saw 9/11 from a different perspective. A "Turkish lad" slashing a bird's foot was not totally unfamiliar to me. Though I had no sympathy for wanton rage, coming from the East I could understand how it might arise more easily than Westerners. Irrationality was as irritating to me as to any other creature of a Cartesian culture, but as a native of the Danube basin, I found it less puzzling. I could also entertain the politically incorrect notion that we might be at war, not just with "terrorism" in general, but with the specific terrorism of Islam.

Perhaps Muslim resentment and rage should not have come as a surprise to anyone. Western ascendancy had been rubbing salt into the wounds of Islamic decline for centuries. As the Princeton scholar Bernard Lewis observed in 1990:

> For a long time now there has been a rising tide of rebellion against this Western paramountcy, and a desire to reassert Muslim values and restore Muslim greatness. The Muslim has suffered successive stages of defeat. The first was his loss of domination in the world, to the advancing power of Russia and the West. The second was the undermining of his

authority in his own country, through an invasion of foreign ideas and laws and ways of life and sometimes even foreign rulers or settlers, and the enfranchisement of native non-Muslim elements. The third—the last straw—was the challenge to his mastery in his own house, from emancipated women and rebellious children. It was too much to endure, and the outbreak of rage against these alien, infidel, and incomprehensible forces that had subverted his dominance, disrupted his society, and finally violated the sanctuary of his home was inevitable. It was also natural that this rage should be directed primarily against the millennial enemy and should draw its strength from ancient beliefs and loyalties.

For radical Islam, this millennial enemy was not only America or Israel, but the entire "House of War," the world of non-Islamic beliefs and values in general, and Western beliefs and values in particular. The countries of Europe could not exempt themselves from this jihadist view by conciliatory gestures. Neither could Canada.

Stork, stork, *ciconia*,
What makes your foot bleed?

The answer had slammed into the Twin Towers on the morning of September 11, 2001.

George Jonas is the author of fourteen books, including the international bestsellers *Vengeance* and *By Persons Unknown* with Barbara Amiel, as well as his novel *Final Decree* and a memoir, *Beethoven's Mask*. Currently, he writes two weekly columns, one for the *National Post* and another in syndication for CanWest News Service. His columns and articles have appeared in the *National Review, The Chicago Sun-Times, The Daily Telegraph,* and *The Wall Street Journal,* and have been collected and published as books. He has written, produced, and directed over two hundred dramas and docudramas for the CBC, including the award-winning series *The Scales of Justice*. His media awards in Canada and abroad include the Edgar Allan Poe Award for the Best Crime Non-Fiction Book, two Nelly Awards for the Best Radio Program, a National Magazine Award, and two Gemini Awards for the Best TV Movie and for the Best Short Dramatic Program. George Jonas and his wife live in Toronto.